TrimTabs
Investing

Founded in 1807, John Wiley & Sons is the oldest independent publishing company in the United States. With offices in North America, Europe, Australia, and Asia, Wiley is globally committed to developing and marketing print and electronic products and services for our customers' professional and personal knowledge and understanding.

The Wiley Finance series contains books written specifically for finance and investment professionals as well as sophisticated individual investors and their financial advisors. Book topics range from portfolio management to e-commerce, risk management, financial engineering, valuation, and financial instrument analysis, as well as much more.

For a list of available titles, visit our Web site at www.WileyFinance.com.

TrimTabs Investing

Using Liquidity Theory to Beat the Stock Market

CHARLES BIDERMAN
with
DAVID SANTSCHI

WILEY

John Wiley & Sons, Inc.

Published by John Wiley & Sons, Inc., Hoboken, New Jersey.
Published simultaneously in Canada.

For general information on our other products and services, or technical support, please contact our Customer Care Department within the United States at 800-762-2974, outside the United States at 317-572-3993 or fax 317-572-4002.

Wiley also publishes its books in a variety of electronic formats. Some content that appears in print may not be available in electronic books. For more information about Wiley products, visit our web site at www.wiley.com.

Library of Congress Cataloging-in-Publication Data:
Biderman, Charles, 1946–
   TrimTabs investing : using liquidity theory to beat the stock market / Charles Biderman with David Santschi.
      p.   cm. — (Wiley finance series)
   ISBN 0-471-69720-6 (CLOTH)
   1. Stocks.   2. Stocks—United States.   3. Liquidity (Economics)   4. Investment analysis.   5. Stock exchanges—United States.   I. Santschi, David.   II. Title.   III. Series.
      HG4661.B53   2005
      332.63'22—dc22

                                                           2004024582

Printed in the United States of America.

10 9 8 7 6 5 4 3 2 1

Dedication

To the possibility of global prosperity.

Contents

Acknowledgments

While family always comes first, it is not acknowledged nearly enough. My two boys, J.P. and Chris, are my sources of joy and adventure, and they had to put up with a lot growing up. Thank you for your love. I thank my sister, Naomi Allen, her husband, Jeffrey, and their daughters, Rebecca and Jennifer, who have always been there for me. I owe particular acknowledgment to my two ex-wives, who loved me completely even though I never knew why at the time. My cousin, Joseph Mandrowitz, deserves acknowledgment for surviving the Holocaust and continuing to live a full life despite the horrors and disappointments he has experienced.

After family comes work. I acknowledge each member of the TrimTabs Investment Research cohort: Michael Alexander, Grace Billings, Rich Gibson, Keith Nielsen, Paul Nugent, Mike Piken, C. J. Puffer, David Santschi, Madeline Schnapp, and Carl Wittnebert. They are responsible for the good stuff. Anything that has not worked is my fault. I am also grateful to TrimTabs' brilliant clients. I would not have a business without them.

I owe my career in part to the Harvard Business School admissions officer who accepted my application. I still have not figured out why Harvard admitted a C+ student from Brooklyn College.

Alan Abelson deserves kudos for hiring a nonwriter who admittedly could read a balance sheet from the footnotes forward. Many successful Wall Street players owe an enormous debt to Alan for his support over the years.

Meyer Berman—wherever you are—thank you. Meyer took me in when I left *Barron's*. He not only gave me a desk and a phone, he gave me his contacts, including a relationship with the brilliant lawyer Andy Garr. When I founded TrimTabs, Meyer stepped up to become my first client.

After obtaining everything I ever thought I wanted in sex and money by the age of 30, I realized I knew less than nothing about life. I owe a great deal to the people who taught me, including Ole Larsen, Robert Monroe, Jack Schwarz, Buckminster Fuller, Michael Murphy, and Werner Erhard. For 10 years, I volunteered at Werner Erhard and Associates, where I learned about the being part of human being.

In writing this book, I particularly thank Maria Bartiromo for introducing me to Wayne Kabak of the William Morris Agency; Debra Englander of John Wiley & Sons; and the staff at Cape Cod Compositors.

David Santschi deserves thanks from all the readers of this book. This book would not have been written if it were not for his ability to turn turgid prose into something fun to read.

—Charles Biderman

I thank my parents, Jan and Tim, for their love and support. I could not have completed this project without them. I also thank my brother, Doug, for being a great friend. My grandmother, Helen Robinson, also deserves acknowledgment. She warned me to watch what "the big boys" were doing in the stock market long before I knew anything about liquidity theory. She also shared her knowledge of the consequences of economic busts. While we merely write about the Great Depression in this book, she lived through it as a teenager in Chicago.

Whatever analytical and writing abilities I possess are due in large measure to good teachers. I thank Peter Ahrensdorf, Robin Barnes, Jonathan Berkey, Suzanne Desan, Vivian Dietz, Rosemary Ennis, Andrew Hope, Carol Ihlendorf, Malcolm Partin, Earl Rudisell, J. Russell Snapp, Johann Sommerville, Lee Palmer Wandel, and T.C. Price Zimmermann for their guidance through the years. They have influenced me more than they probably realize.

This book would not have been possible without the efforts of many dedicated people. I thank Wayne Kabak of the William Morris Agency; Debra Englander, Greg Friedman, and Todd Tedesco of John Wiley & Sons; and the staff at Cape Cod Compositors for all of their hard work. Judy Steenstra of the Investment Company Institute and Rich Gibson, Madeline Schnapp, and Carl Wittnebert of TrimTabs Investment Research were a great help in gathering the data used in this book.

Finally, I thank Charles Biderman and Madeline Schnapp for sharing their wisdom, both financial and otherwise. I am grateful to them for taking a chance on a historian without a degree in economics. It has been a lot of fun.

—David Santschi

TrimTabs Investing

Introduction

At your local bookstore, you can probably find dozens of books about the stock market. In fact, scores of investing titles roll off the presses every year. When you picked up this book, you may well have glanced at the jacket and thought, "Who is this guy? And why does he think the world needs another book about the stock market?"

My name is Charles Biderman. I am the founder and president of TrimTabs Investment Research. For the past 10 years, TrimTabs has been developing liquidity theory, a unique paradigm for understanding the stock market. Nearly all of TrimTabs' clients are institutional investors, including portfolio managers and hedge fund managers on the buy side and market strategists on the sell side. I owe a great deal to our clients for their insights in developing liquidity theory. In my admittedly biased opinion, they are some of the smartest investors on Wall Street.

BEATING THE STOCK MARKET CASINO

The first reason I am writing this book is to show sophisticated investors how to use liquidity theory to beat the stock market casino. Unfortunately for me, however, most investors do not need this book. Before I discuss why I am writing this book for sophisticated investors, everyone else can learn how to beat the stock market casino in the next few paragraphs.

Anyone with a salary and a willingness to save money can beat the stock market casino in one of two simple ways. The first is dollar-cost averaging. Dollar-cost averaging means investing a fixed amount of cash into the stock market on a regular basis regardless of stock market fluctuations. Dollar-cost averaging allows investors to participate in the continuing growth of the U.S. economy. An investor who began investing $100 each month into the S&P 200—the precursor of the S&P 500—at the end of December 1929 and continued to do so for 10 years would have earned a profit of 12.7 percent on his $12,000 investment (not deducting commissions nor adding the compounding benefit of dividend reinvestment) after 10 years even though the S&P 200 dropped 50 percent over this period. Indeed, if an investor continued investing $100 in the S&P 500 each month through 1959, his $36,000 would have more than quadrupled to $145,900. If this $145,900 were left untouched until today, the original $36,000 would be worth $2,436,132 (not deducting taxes nor adding the compounding benefit of dividend reinvestment) with the S&P 500 at 1,000. The original $36,000 would be worth $2,679,746 with the S&P 500 at 1,100.

For full disclosure, both of my sons dollar-cost average into the Vanguard 500 Index fund, which has an expense ratio of just 0.18 percent. Investors who wish to do nothing more than dollar-cost average into the stock market do not need to read this book any further.

However, the reality is that very few people dollar-cost average. My older son stopped dollar-cost averaging in early 2002 without telling me because the stock market had been grinding downward for nearly two years. After I yelled at him, he resumed dollar-cost averaging, and his portfolio weathered the bear market quite well. While dollar-cost averaging is a foolproof way to make money in the stock market, most investors do not dollar-cost average. Instead, they actively trade their stock holdings, even though academic studies have shown that most investors lose money trading in the stock market. Often these investors blame their losses on bad luck. They are indeed unlucky—if you consider people who lose money in casinos to be unlucky!

The second simple way to make money in the stock market is to buy the stocks of great companies and hold them forever, reaping the rewards of compound interest. Buy-and-hold investors should always heed the old Wall Street adage: "Never confuse wisdom with a bull market." The U.S. stock market first opened for business at the end of the eighteenth century. Since that time, the U.S. economy has grown more quickly than any other economy in the history of the planet. Investing in the U.S. stock market by buying a reasonable number of stocks in quality companies and holding them for several generations has created many a large fortune. Even at rates as low as 5 percent, compound interest turns a modest amount of money into an enormous amount of wealth over the course of a century. For example, an initial sum of $20,000 compounded monthly at 5 percent interest over 100 years would grow to $2,937,589, excluding the effects of inflation and taxes.

Buy-and-hold investors whose stock holdings have swelled to become a fortune are often mistaken about why they are successful. While they often boast about their investing prowess, the 200-year bull market driven by the record-setting U.S. economy is actually responsible for their success. In other words, they confuse wisdom with a bull market. Many investors who began playing the stock market casino in the late 1990s buying Internet start-ups on tips from friends or brokers lost nearly all of their money. Yet investors who did their homework and bought a basket of good quality companies even though at inflated prices—such as Amazon.com, Cisco Systems, eBay, Intel, Johnson & Johnson, Pfizer, Wal-Mart, and Yahoo!—will probably do all right if they hang on to their holdings for the next generation or so.

Liquidity theory is designed for sophisticated investors who want to achieve higher returns than those available through dollar-cost averaging or buying and holding the stocks of great companies. As this book explains, liquidity theory holds that the stock market is no different from the market for any other good. As in other markets, stock prices are set by supply and demand, not fundamental value. In other words, stock prices do not change based on changes in expected future earnings, as most people on Wall Street claim. Instead, they are determined by changes in the number of shares in the stock market and the amount of money available to buy them. Liquidity theory uses this information to predict the direction of the stock market.

This book details a unique investment strategy not explained in other books. Whether you are a hedge fund manager with $250 million in assets under management or an individual investor with a small nest egg, this book shows you how to put the power of liquidity theory to work in your portfolio. Assuming the U.S. economy continues to grow between 3 percent and 6 percent annually over the next few decades (and I will discuss below why I believe this level of growth is quite realistic) investors who follow liquidity theory will likely amass great fortunes over time. How can I be so sure? TrimTabs clients who have invested according to liquidity theory have trounced the major stock market averages over the past decade.

PROMOTING GLOBAL PROSPERITY

Yet this book is not merely a guide to achieving higher returns in the stock market. I am also writing it to promote global prosperity, which currently faces two main threats: bad leaders and economic busts. By prosperity, I mean not only the ability of an economy to generate a surplus of calories for its members but also the ability of its members to produce and consume other desirable goods and services. Prosperity is primarily a function of communication. From prehistory through the twentieth century, every breakthrough in communication has created a breakthrough in wealth creation. People who first mastered the use of horses and chariots conquered their neighbors and became significantly more prosperous. The Romans constructed roads to expedite the passage of military units, which helped create the world's first regional empire. The Middle Ages ended with the development of the printing press and improved navigational techniques. Steam railroads were another major breakthrough in communication, as the ability to bring food to cities from distant agricultural regions created a huge increase in per capita calorie consumption. With the development of the first gasoline-powered automobiles more than 100 years ago, the ability to transport goods multiplied, further increasing per capita calorie consumption. About 50 years ago, airplanes, television, and the interstate highway system came of age. All of these communication breakthroughs created breakthroughs in wealth creation.

The beneficial effects of these communication breakthroughs were limited mainly to first world and second world countries. In the nineteenth and twentieth centuries, societies with representative governments that least interfered with the adoption of communication breakthroughs—meaning they did not nationalize innovations such as railroads, telephones, and television for the financial benefit of rulers—experienced the greatest breakthroughs in per capita calorie consumption.

Threat One: Bad Leaders

Why were third world countries excluded from many of the communication breakthroughs that allowed inhabitants of first world and second world countries to live well above subsistence level? The answer is simple: bad leaders. Few people understand that third world rulers treat their state treasuries as their personal checking accounts and that the design purpose of third world governments is to maintain the power of their existing rulers. Third world countries are ruled by an elite that controls business, government, labor, the military, and organized crime. For the record, organized crime exists only when governments create laws about personal morality (e.g., denying individuals the opportunities to kill themselves using drugs, cigarettes, and alcohol; pay for sex; or borrow money at usurious interest rates with only body parts as collateral). As the world moves further toward consumer capitalism, organized crime seems to decline.

There is little any book can do about bad leaders. Fortunately the rise of the Internet has made the global economy even more tightly integrated, which makes it more difficult for bad leaders to remain in power today than at any time in the past. The longer bad leaders can limit the access of their citizens to the Internet, the longer they can stay in power. Indeed, the prosperity the Internet is creating throughout the world is leading to what I call the Age of the Common Man—an age in which all people can receive sufficient calories each day so that old age rather than malnutrition will be the major cause of death. In the 1990s, the Internet created the possibility of a world in which every e-mail address is the equal of every other e-mail address in the ability to consume or provide goods and services. This development has occurred regardless of the complaints of those who rail against the outsourcing of services from the United States to countries where people consume a fraction of the goods and services Americans do.

The form of society being fostered by the Internet is what I call consumer capitalism. I define consumer capitalism as a political and economic system in which the interests of consumers take precedence over the elites of business, government, labor, the military, and organized crime. For example, a company like Wal-Mart can exist only in a system of consumer capitalism because of the devastation it wreaks on the local retailers where it does business. You may be wondering why I include labor in the list of organizations controlled by elites. While organized labor initially developed to represent the common man, after a few decades labor union leaders began to have more in common with their counterparts in business and government than they did with the common man.

The best term to describe the older form of government in which the same people control business, government, labor, the military, and organized crime is fascism. Currently China, India, Japan, Mexico, Russia, South Korea, most countries in Latin America, and some countries in Europe are fascist states. Fascist states are concerned for the welfare of the ruling class first and everyone else last. For example, Mario Monti, the European Union's Commissioner for Competition, prohibited General Electric from taking over Honeywell in 2001. In that case, the interests of a few European companies trumped the benefits that would accrue from this deal to European consumers.

To highlight the distinction between consumer capitalism and fascism, consider Wal-Mart and Microsoft. Fascist elites despise Wal-Mart because it hurts local businesses even as it benefits the great mass of consumers. People who fight Wal-Mart, which is a major driver of consumer capitalism, use fascist arguments to protect elites despite the benefits Wal-Mart offers everyone else. By contrast, Microsoft in its current form is an enemy of consumer capitalism because it wishes to control access to the Internet, just as many governments do when the Internet begins to threaten their sovereignty. In this way, Microsoft behaves far more like a Japanese or a French company than an American one.

Many fascist states are currently evolving toward consumer capitalism. In these states, wealth is shifting from an elite ruling class toward those who provide the most and the best goods and services for everyone else. India and Russia are excellent examples of how formerly closed countries are benefiting from a shift toward consumer capitalism. Take a look at Figure I.1, which compares the Bombay Sensex and the Moscow Times against the S&P 500 from July 1997 to July 2004. Note in particular the explosive

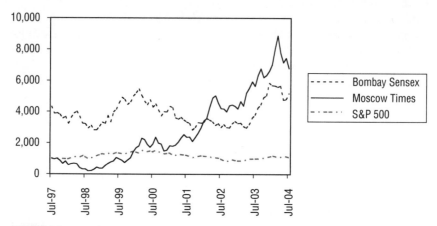

FIGURE I.1   Bombay Sensex, Moscow Times, and S&P 500, July 1997 to July 2004
Raw data obtained from Yahoo! Finance.

returns of the Bombay Sensex and the Moscow Times compared to the S&P 500 since late 2002.

As consumers in fascist countries create enough wealth for themselves to be able to replace laws protecting government, business, and labor elites with laws protecting consumers, they sow the seeds of fascism's destruction. Once property rights, free markets, and personal freedom take hold, the economies of formerly fascist states usually boom.

Threat Two: Economic Busts

Unfortunately, economic busts typically follow economic booms, and these economic busts are the second main threat to global prosperity. To prevent global economic busts from derailing the great wealth creation currently occurring around the world, the upside potential of economic booms needs to be limited. I believe TrimTabs played a small role in preventing the technology boom of the late 1990s from growing even larger than it did, but it is Alan Greenspan who is owed a major debt of gratitude by all consumers. Even though millions of Americans lost trillions of dollars on paper in the stock market during the boom, the bust did not bankrupt a single major U.S. financial institution. That happy outcome has never occurred during a previous economic bust or stock market bust.

Liquidity theory can help prevent stock market booms from reaching such heights that the resulting busts wipe out banks and investors, causing economic disaster. Frank Fernandez, the much-underappreciated senior economist of the U.S. Securities Industry Association (SIA), was working with TrimTabs to develop a weekly TrimTabs/SIA Liquidity Index to track booms and prevent them from raging out of control. One of the results of the September 11 terrorist attacks was a reduction in the SIA's budget, which prevented us from collaborating. Nevertheless, a world in which more people are reaping the benefits of global consumer capitalism and in which economic booms and busts are more limited is a world heading toward widespread prosperity. Amen.

HONORING MY PARENTS

Finally, I am writing this book for a personal reason. My parents, Jacob Jeruzalski Biderman and Pauline Youngerman, were Holocaust survivors. Their prior spouses and three of their children, my half-brothers and half-sister, did not survive the Holocaust, and the memories of that horror haunted my parents for the rest of their lives. My mother's first cousin and only other close relative to survive the Holocaust, Joseph Mandrowitz, was imprisoned in about 10 concentration camps during World War II. To this day, he says the smell from the crematoria is with him daily. To honor my parents, I am driven to help create a world without holocausts.

Introducing Liquidity Theory

CHAPTER 1

A Tale of Fortune Lost

Judy Wei thought she had hit pay dirt. The $6,000 that she had invested in a handful of technology stocks was growing like a magic beanstalk. Her investment club's portfolio was leaving the S&P 500 in the dust. And the analysts who paraded before CNBC's cameras gave her every reason to believe that the best was yet to come. For the first time in her memory, Judy allowed herself to believe that everything was finally going to work out all right.

The incredible position in which Judy found herself was about as far from her humble upbringing in Taiwan as she could imagine. It was also her ultimate vindication—her cousins and friends back in Taiwan had long warned her against immigrating to the United States. She would slowly lose contact with her culture, they argued, and she would receive little in return. Did she have any idea of the discrimination that she would face? "I didn't believe any of them. I felt in my heart this was right," Judy recalls. Finally she drew up the courage to pursue her dream. She spent all of her modest savings to move to California. Shortly after her arrival, she lived in a four-by-seven-foot bedroom in an East Palo Alto apartment that friends of her family rented to her. She quickly found a job in a cafeteria at Stanford University. There she met her future husband, Chun, a lanky law student who burned with ambition. Together they struggled to make a life for themselves. Chun eventually landed work at a chip equipment company in San Jose, while Judy raised their three daughters.

As her husband was rapidly promoted, Judy began to believe more fervently in the American dream. Even immigrants who arrived with nothing could prosper in the land of opportunity, she thought. Once her daughters grew older and went off to college, Judy found herself with more free time. Her husband, though, was consumed by his work. Often he would spend seven days a week at the office, and he hardly ever took vacation time. Since he no longer had time to manage the family finances, Judy gradually assumed this responsibility.

Soon she became captivated by the stock market. A few of her friends—some of the same people who had warned her not to immigrate to America but had eventually followed her—told stories of financing a second home by riding to immense heights the stock of CMGI, an Internet-advertising company. One friend took a low-ranking marketing job at Qualcomm. After two years, he was contemplating retirement because the paper value of his stock options had skyrocketed. "One of my friends said, 'If you have no money in Internet stocks in November 1999, you're going to become a second-class citizen in just a few months,'" Judy says. It seemed that almost anyone could turn a few thousand dollars into a fortune in a matter of weeks or even days.

Judy realized that she knew little about the stock market, so she took a cautious approach. She joined an investment club patterned on the Beardstown Ladies. By February 2000, the club had turned its $15,000 initial investment into $63,500. As for the future, the sky was the limit. Judy's group was confident that its superior stock picking would beat the market averages with ease. Of course, it helped that one of the club members was married to a chief financial officer (CFO) at a fiber optics start-up that had been bought out by Cisco Systems. The club pumped much of its money into the hottest telecommunications stocks following the wisdom of Salomon Smith Barney analyst named Jack Grubman. Judy was told that Grubman could send a stock's price soaring just by recommending it. Judy had never watched much television, but after she joined the investment club, she kept her television tuned to CNBC as she cleaned the house, did crossword puzzles, and chatted with friends.

Worried that she had entered the market too late, Judy took a financial plunge as risky as her move from Taiwan to California. She decided to invest $700,000 of her family's assets into technology stocks. This sum was everything they owned except their house, $30,000 that they had vowed never to touch except in an emergency, and $6,000 that they were planning to use for a trip back to Taiwan that summer. Awash in options at his company, Chun agreed with her decision.

Judy and Chun hardly worried when the Nasdaq began to lose steam in March 2000. "We all thought, stocks have dropped down like this before, but they always went on to new highs," Judy remembers. She and her husband agreed that the most successful investors always invest for the long term. Moreover, telecom stocks were weathering the storm relatively well, so Judy and Chun thought they might fare better than stocks in other sectors. By the end of 2000, however, doubts were creeping into Judy's mind. Stock in Chun's employer had plunged 76 percent. Most of Chun's stock options had become worthless, and the rest of them would soon be submerged if the market continued to decline. But Judy had invested too much of her savings to back out at a loss. She held firm, hoping that the brighter days of late 1999 and early 2000 would return.

Not until the terrorist attacks of September 11, 2001, did Judy feel certain that she had to get out of the market no matter what the cost. She had lost nearly $500,000 of her family's life savings. This sum included the money that Judy and Chun had reserved for seeing their daughters through graduate school. The Nasdaq had fallen about 70 percent from its peak, and the television pundits were now predicting that the bottom was nowhere in sight. "It was the hardest thing I ever had to do," Judy says. She liquidated all of her stock holdings. Once the market bottomed, she thought, she would get fully invested again and profit from the rebound.

In the months after Judy liquidated her holdings, reality hit hard. Jack Grubman, the analyst who had been ushered into the inner circle of countless telecom firms, was being investigated for conflicts of interest. Regulators alleged that he had grown so close to companies that he covered that he had helped them at the expense of small investors like Judy and her investment club. Grubman was not the only analyst putting lipstick on pigs to generate investment banking revenue for his firm. Famed Internet analyst Henry Blodget left Merrill Lynch in exchange for a $2 million buyout shortly after the September 11 attacks. He had issued glowing recommendations on stocks of companies that had investment banking relationships with his firm even when he believed that they were poor investments. Most memorably, Blodget maintained the equivalent of a "buy" rating on 24/7 Real Media while conceding to another analyst that the stock was a "piece of shit." Some of Blodget's other recommendations, most notably eToys and Pets.com, went out of business after the bubble burst. As part of a $1.4 billion settlement with leading Wall Street brokerage firms in April 2003, Grubman and Blodget agreed to pay a total of $19 million in fines and be permanently barred from the securities industry.

Analysts were not the only subjects of scrutiny. Once the bubble burst, the dirty laundry that had been concealed or ignored for years was finally hauled out into the open. Senior executives such as Bernard Ebbers and Scott Sullivan at WorldCom, Kenneth Lay and Jeffrey Skilling at Enron, and Gary Winnick at Global Crossing were accused of various corrupt practices. New York Attorney General Eliot Spitzer launched an investigation, based in part on daily mutual fund flow data provided by TrimTabs Investment Research, that uncovered irregularities at a host of major mutual fund companies, including Alger, Invesco, Janus, Putnam, and Strong. Some of these companies allowed favored clients to perform rapid-fire trades in their mutual funds even while they prohibited ordinary investors from doing the same. Others allowed hedge funds to buy and sell mutual funds after 4:00 P.M. and still receive that day's closing price, a practice that their mutual funds' prospectuses explicitly prohibited. Richard Strong, who founded Strong Financial Corporation in 1974, was forced to resign from his own company's board amid allegations that he generated hundreds of thousands of dollars in profits by improperly trading his own company's mutual funds. Eventually Strong settled federal and state allegations against him by paying $60 million in fines and restitution, publicly apologizing to investors, and agreeing to be barred from the securities industry for life. Yet Judy stopped paying attention to these developments. After she sold her stocks in the wake of the September 11 attacks, she tuned out CNBC and canceled all of her subscriptions to financial magazines. She hardly even glanced at the business section of her local newspaper. The parade of corruption that dominated the headlines of the financial press made her sick.

Nearly three years later, Judy and Chun have their remaining assets parked in a savings account at their local bank that earns less than 1 percent interest. When the S&P 500 dropped to around 800 during October 2002 and again during March 2003, Judy refused to consider investing in the stock market. In fact, she remains unwilling to invest her money in any vehicle that would expose their remaining savings to even the slightest loss. Chun has been issued new stock options, but he plans to retire in a few years. Unless the market suddenly explodes, the couple's nest egg will be modest. Chun hopes that it will be enough to see them through their golden years. But he adds, "This will be a different retirement than we had planned." They never expected to rely on Social Security for nearly half of their retirement income.

A FAMILIAR TALE

Over the past few years, the carnage of the technology bubble spread to nearly every community in America, and stories like Judy's played out for millions of families. More than $7 trillion in wealth evaporated during the brutal bear market of 2000–2002, and much of it was held by ordinary Americans. Carefree retirements, educations at prestigious universities, vacation homes—many of these dreams were dashed or dramatically scaled back after the largest financial bubble in world history burst. At Enron and WorldCom alone, tens of thousands of employees who had staked their retirements on their pension plans with these firms were left with practically nothing.

The seven months between October 1999 and April 2000 were a remarkable period in the history of U.S. financial markets. The technology bubble peaked on March 10, 2000, when the Nasdaq hit an all-time high of 5,132.52. During these seven months, investors like Judy poured an astonishing $182 billion—more than $26 billion per month—into U.S. equity mutual funds and probably at least as much into individual stocks directly. Much of this cash flowed into technology and Internet darlings like Cisco Systems, Yahoo!, and JDS Uniphase. Investors valued Internet companies according to novel measures like "clicks per hour," and they earnestly compared the relative merits of various "B2C" (business to consumer) and "B2B" (business to business) plays. At the same time between the end of October 1999 and the end of March 2000, margin debt levels at New York Stock Exchange member firms surged an astonishing $96 billion—an average of almost $20 billion per month—as investors borrowed money to buy stocks, convinced that the economic boom of the 1990s would keep right on rolling into the new millennium.

The stock market captivated the nation as never before. Tens of thousands of people quit their jobs to become full-time day traders, jumping in and out of stocks in an attempt to profit from short-term price fluctuations. Hundreds of thousands of other investors from all walks of life—auto mechanics, lawyers, graduate students, homemakers—regularly tuned in to CNBC to follow the latest pronouncements of star analysts. Stock tips and speculation about the stock market were the subject of conversations at cocktail parties and offices alike. Many people were just waiting until their stock options unlocked and they, too, could get out and enjoy the good life. It seemed that the boom would never end. Eventually, like all booms, it did end. Some investors escaped with significant but manageable losses. Others were not so fortunate and were completely wiped out.

The excesses of the technology bubble are well known. But what exactly was corporate America doing in the stock market during this period? The answer is highly revealing. Beginning in late 1999, corporate America began buying back fewer shares of stock than it sold. The heights reached by the major market averages prompted an epidemic of corporate vertigo. While CEOs complained about a lack of earnings visibility, CFOs took action and clamped down on share buybacks. Why repurchase shares if a downturn was imminent? Not only did companies repurchase fewer of their own shares, the incredible demand for stock prompted them to unload as many new shares as they could. While the financial media lavished the most attention on initial public offerings (IPOs), the bulk of the money was being raised in secondary offerings. In other words, companies that were already public, such as Sun Microsystems, sold billions in additional shares to eager investors. The sharp decline in stock buybacks, accompanied by the surge in new offerings, was a dramatic shift from the period from 1994 through October 1999, when corporate America bought far more shares of stock than it sold.

But these warnings from public companies themselves were drowned out by the din of cheerleading analysts and journalists. Few stock market investors, least of all investment clubs like Judy's, were paying any attention to what corporate insiders were doing. Instead, they were too busy listening to the latest recommendations from Wall Street analysts, who counseled that the stock market had entered a "new era" of handsome returns driven by computer technology. We all know how those predictions played out.

LIQUIDITY THEORY: A NEW PARADIGM

What is particularly tragic about an experience like Judy's is that it need not have occurred. If Judy had paid more attention to the actions of corporate America than she did to the opinions of Wall Street analysts, she might have been able to realize her dreams and protect her family's assets. The fundamental principle of our investment approach, which we call liquidity theory, is quite simple: *to beat the stock market casino, invest the way that public companies and corporate insiders do.* In other words, buy stocks when corporate America is buying and sell stocks when corporate America is selling. Contrary to what the vast majority of investment professionals claim, the best leading indicator of the performance of the stock market is not stock valuations, earnings growth, or chart patterns. It is the collective actions of corporate investors—both public companies and the insiders who run them—in the stock market. Why? Because public companies and the insiders who run them are the smart money in the stock market casino. We also follow another principle: *Be aware of what individual and institutional investors are doing.* Even if corporate America is a net seller, the market can rise if investors are buying heavily enough to offset corporate America's sales. Conversely, even if corporate America is a net buyer, the market can fall if investors are selling heavily enough to offset corporate America's purchases. Investors are the dumb money in the stock market. As will we see, they invariably buy high and sell low. Their actions are a useful contrary indicator, particularly when they become extreme.

If Judy and millions of other investors had followed liquidity theory, they would not only have been spared the agonies of the bear market of 2000–2002, but they also would have been able to profit when the market bottomed in late 2002 and early 2003. How do we know? Because we did exactly that. From September 2000—when in our liquidity formula we began separating corporate buying and selling from U.S. equity mutual fund inflows—through December 2004, our model futures portfolio increased 115 percent (unaudited), while the S&P 500 declined 16 percent.

Our original $100,000 paper model portfolio, which began on July 12, 1993, has grown to $1,482,051 (unaudited) as of December 31, 2004, a gain of 1,382 percent. For comparison, the S&P 500 rose just 171 percent over the same period.

We did not achieve these results through rapid-fire trading. On average, we trade the holdings in our model portfolio two times per month.

We did not achieve these results by picking the next hot stocks or sectors. Our model portfolio uses only stock index futures, and we make no attempt to pick stocks or sectors.

We did not achieve these results using complex strategies or exotic investment vehicles. Individual investors could easily replicate our model portfolio with just a few exchange-traded funds.

So how did we achieve these results? We applied liquidity theory in a disciplined way to the stock market. In other words, we beat the stock market casino by buying and selling according to changes in stock market liquidity.

Liquidity theory can be used by anyone who manages money. It is obviously relevant to the work of investment professionals, such as portfolio managers and market strategists. Yet it is equally appropriate for individual investors who manage their own money. Given the decline in defined-benefit retirement plans over the past 20 years, this group includes an increasing proportion of the U.S. population. According to "equity ownership in America," a study conducted by the Investment Company Institute and the Securities Industry Association in 2002, 49.5 percent of all U.S. households owned stocks in 2002—a sharp increase from 36.6 percent in 1992 and 19.0 percent in 1983. As we will show in this book, anyone capable of accumulating significant sums of cash is capable of managing his or her own assets. Managing money effectively is not all that difficult.

Nevertheless, a significant proportion of individual investors have curtailed their investments following steep losses in the 2000–2002 bear market, revelations of lazy oversight by regulators, and a daisy chain of scandals involving brokerage firms and mutual fund companies. Many individual investors became convinced not only that the stock market is rigged against the small investor but that they have little chance of even earning a decent return on their investments. If you are one of these individuals and you are looking for a smart way back into the stock market, this book may be for you.

Quite frankly, however, many investors do not need this book. If you wish to invest for long-term goals and have no interest in learning about financial markets or investments, we recommend that you simply dollar-cost average into Vanguard index funds. Dollar-cost averaging means investing the same amount of money at regular intervals into the market without regard for market conditions. Vanguard index funds offer broad exposure to various asset classes—including stocks, bonds, precious metals, and real estate—at some of the lowest costs in the financial services industry. A diversified portfolio of Vanguard index funds will also likely outperform the vast majority of professional money managers. We believe that fewer than 200 money managers are able to outperform the market consistently, and many of these exceptional managers will not even accept your money. Even if you begin dollar-cost averaging at the worst possible time, you will likely make money over the long haul. For instance, if you had dollar-cost averaged into the market from the end of 1929 to 1939—the worst decade ever for the U.S. stock market—you would have earned a 12.7 percent return despite the Great Depression. The U.S. economy has grown faster than any other economy in world history, and its strong performance is likely to continue. Dollar-cost averaging into Vanguard index funds will ensure that your portfolio participates in the economy's long-term growth.

If, however, you are interested in handling your portfolio more professionally and actively managing it to achieve higher returns, then this book is for you. Regardless of the size of your portfolio, you can successfully implement liquidity-based strategies if you are willing to invest the time to learn how the stock market casino works.

We also hope this book will do more than simply show investors how to profit from investments in the stock market. We are also writing to advance a series of simple, low-cost proposals that would require greater disclosure of corporate transactions. Armed with knowledge of liquidity theory and the information that these proposals would provide, investors would be far less likely to pour money into the stock market during bubbles—when corporate America is selling—and abandon stocks during bear markets—when corporate America is buying. As a result, market volatility would decline, and the busts that inevitably follow booms would not be nearly as severe. It is the bankruptcies that inevitably accompany busted bubbles—not stock market losses themselves—that can wreak havoc on economies and societies.

For example, bankruptcies and bank failures, not the stock market crash, were the primary causes of the Great Depression. According to the U.S. Department of Agriculture, net farm income plunged from $7.8 billion in 1920 to $3.4 billion in 1921, and it recovered only gradually to $6.2 billion by 1929. As a result, many farmers could no longer afford to pay their mortgages, and an average of 70 banks failed each year during the 1920s. Once the stock market crashed, banks that speculated on equities without adequate reserves were ruined. In fact, an average of 900 banks failed each year during the 1930s. By the time President Franklin Delano Roosevelt was inaugurated in March 1933, banks in every state had closed or restricted the amount of cash that depositors could withdraw. Since no deposit insurance existed, bank failures caused many depositors to lose much of their life savings. Business transactions were increasingly conducted by barter, and the hoarding of gold was so widespread that President Roosevelt signed an executive order prohibiting it in April 1933. As a result of bank failures and bankruptcies, economic activity contracted sharply. According to the U.S. Bureau of the Census, the unemployment rate for nonagricultural workers exceeded 25 percent from 1931 to 1936, and it surpassed 35 percent from late 1931 to mid-1933. Tens of thousands of men rode the rails, traveling from place to place searching for whatever work they could find. Families scrounged to reduce expenses, and standards of living plummeted even as much of the machinery used to produce essential goods sat idle. By 1932, median income and industrial production were only half of what they had been in 1929. While not everyone stood in bread lines or lived in shantytowns, everyone was affected by the economic collapse, and the United States did not pull out of its economic funk until it became involved in World War II. Many Americans who lived through the Great Depression avoided the stock market for the rest of their lives.

We are not predicting another Great Depression. Monetary policy and financial instruments designed to prevent illiquidity are much more sophisticated now than they were 75 years ago. In fact, not a single bank failed during the collapse of the technology bubble in 2000–2002. Yet the economic consequences of the resulting bust were still severe. Tens of thousands of businesses failed, millions of people lost their jobs, and tens of millions of others lost confidence in corporate America and the financial markets. Like Judy, many investors who were badly burned have yet to return to the stock market. We contend that wider use of liquidity theory would mean lower highs and higher lows for the stock market. By limiting the scale of booms, widespread adoption of liquidity theory would also limit the ensuing busts that are so destructive to the economy. Thus, investors would be more willing to commit capital to the stock market. Reduced volatility would also benefit companies because they would enjoy a steadier flow of capital to develop their businesses, which would in turn encourage more job creation in the U.S. economy. While the boom-bust nature of the financial markets can never be completely eliminated—speculators will always try to push the limits in any market—liquidity theory could at least mitigate market excesses.

AN OVERVIEW

This book begins by describing how Charles Biderman developed the basic principles of liquidity theory in the wake of his own personal bankruptcy. We argue that the stock market is basically a casino in which the house—public companies and the insiders who run them—buys and sells shares with the players—institutional and individual investors. Stock prices in the stock market casino are primarily a function of liquidity—the supply of stock and the demand for it—rather than fundamental value. Then we outline the building blocks of liquidity analysis and show how they can be used to predict the direction of the stock market.

The second part demolishes the conventional Wall Street wisdom that earnings growth drives stock prices. It demonstrates that liquidity carries far more predictive power in the stock market casino than value investing. In further chapters, we show how investors can track the components of liquidity theory using readily available sources, including Internet sites and financial newspapers. Drawing on years of experience in analyzing stock market liquidity, we explain how investors can use these components to beat the stock market casino.

The third part takes a look back at the past 10 years of stock market history. During this period, investors experienced an astonishing range of market conditions, from a secular bull market to a bubble to a brutal bear market to a tentative recovery. This section focuses on liquidity conditions during these tumultuous years and how they influenced the direction of the stock market. It does not simply dwell upon how followers of liquidity theory should have invested during this period. After all, hindsight is always 20/20. Instead, it discusses the actual calls that we made in our model futures portfolio. For example, we explain how we achieved a 74 percent return in our model portfolio during 2002 even as most investors were being mauled by the bear market.

The fourth part explains how investors of all levels of wealth and experience—from individual investors just beginning an investment program to seasoned institutional investors—can put the power of liquidity theory to work in their portfolios. We detail a series of strategies, which range from highly conservative to extremely aggressive, that use liquidity theory to beat the stock market casino.

The fifth part points to the future. It discusses the difficulties that followers of liquidity theory face and offers practical advice on how to manage them. It also explores how new applications in personal income and employment analysis can forecast the amount of cash available for investment in the stock and bond markets. We conclude with a discussion of proposals that would not only improve the transparency of financial markets but also mitigate the boom-bust tendencies of the stock market. We argue that if more near real-time liquidity data were available to investors, U.S. financial markets and the U.S. economy would be much healthier.

As we write this book, no one expects another bubble as massive as the technology bubble of 1999–2000 to emerge anytime soon. Some may even laugh off the excesses of the late 1990s as the foolishness of a bygone era. Yet it would take only a handful of technological breakthroughs to inflate other bubbles in the future. As Warren Buffett quipped at the shareholders meeting of Berkshire Hathaway on May 1, 2004, "What we learn from history is that people don't learn from history." A financial press starved for new trends would be more than willing to trumpet the next "big thing," and the resulting bubble would be no laughing matter after it popped. When it comes along—and it will eventually—liquidity theory will help investors ignore the madness of the crowd and beat the stock market casino.

CHAPTER 2

The Genesis of Liquidity Theory

Charles Biderman began studying money flows in the stock market in 1971, but he did not begin to formulate liquidity theory until 1994. This chapter recounts how liquidity theory developed out of his life's journey and explains some of the lessons—both financial and nonfinancial—he learned along the way.

FROM B-SCHOOL TO *BARRON'S*

After graduating from Harvard Business School, Charles became the associate editor of *Barron's Financial Weekly* from September 1971 to August 1973. He did not get his job in the way most Harvard Business School graduates do. In his first year of business school, Charles helped start a student investment club. In February 1970, the club received a tip about Digital Equipment Corporation from a second-year student who had worked at the company during the summer of 1969. Apparently Digital was warehousing minicomputers for the first time instead of selling them immediately. The Chicago Board Options Exchange did not yet exist, so the group bought out-of-the-money puts on Digital stock that expired in three months. One month passed, but Digital stock did nothing. The club soon figured out that since no one else knew what they knew, the stock would not move.

One afternoon, with several members of the club in his room, Charles had a brainstorm and called Alan Abelson at *Barron's* collect. Surprisingly, Abelson took his call, and Charles told him what he knew about Digital Equipment. Abelson promised to check it out. After Abelson wrote about Digital in *Barron's*, the stock promptly cratered. Charles did not know at the time that Abelson was scheduled to speak that spring at a Harvard Business School finance club event. During Abelson's appearance, Charles promoted himself for a job at *Barron's* in the summer of 1970, and after being persistent in the face of several refusals, he was offered a position that paid $300 per week.

After working for *Barron's* that summer, Charles was invited to work part-time for Abelson during his second year at Harvard and to come on board once he graduated. At *Barron's*, Charles began covering real estate. With New York City investors facing marginal income tax rates of up to 70 percent, real estate offered enormous tax shelter possibilities. Indeed, most of the entrepreneurial action in the 1960s had focused on real estate. During the late 1960s and early 1970s, real estate investment trusts (REITs) became a popular way to fund real estate growth. A real estate bubble eventually formed. In 1973, when the Arab oil embargo began, the bubble began to burst as mortgage interest rates soared from 7 percent in 1972 to between 15 percent and 20 percent by the end of 1973. Due to the doubling of mortgage interest rates, most real estate developments begun in the early 1970s went bust.

RIDING THE REAL ESTATE WAVES

After writing about the impending real estate collapse, Charles left *Barron's*. He had borrowed his way through Harvard Business School, and he had to either earn enough money to pay off his student loans or declare bankruptcy. Meyer Berman, the dean of the Wall Street short-selling community and one source of investment ideas at *Barron's*, gave Charles office space beginning in August 1973. Charles initially recommended that Berman's clients short nearly all of the REITs, since the entire industry was bankrupt.

After the REITs collapsed, Charles recommended buying highly depressed REIT bonds. These bonds traded as low as 5 cents to 10 cents on the dollar, even though the ultimate value of the assets approached par, or $1.00. Then Charles raised capital from a group of investors, who included partners and clients of a major New York City law firm, to buy numerous properties out of foreclosure: 1,000 apartments in Nashville, Tennessee; office buildings in Dallas, Texas, and Memphis, Tennessee; and six strip shopping centers in locations such as Starkville, Mississippi; Fulton, Kentucky; and Milan, Tennessee. In other words, Charles took advantage of the real estate market as it cycled from boom to bust. By the late 1970s, his net worth approached $2 million on paper. He was not yet 35 years old.

Ronald Reagan meant different things to different people. Many people know that he cut taxes dramatically in the early 1980s, lowering the top marginal income tax rate—including state and New York City income taxes—below 45 percent from 70 percent. What many people do not know is that these income tax rate cuts discouraged the smart money from investing in real estate. On the other hand, they made the Internet revolution occur more quickly than it would have otherwise.

During the late 1970s and early 1980s, Charles realized the real estate tax shelter game was over. He also realized that while he had enjoyed tremendous success as a real estate entrepreneur, something was missing from his life. Beginning in 1978, he took a detour through the personal development community. He took all sorts of courses, from Werner Erhard's EST to Ole Larson's Institute of Self Actualization (ISA) to Robert Monroe's course on out-of-body travel to Jack Schwarz's class on aura reading, even ashram hopping in India. The main lesson Charles learned from these courses was that making a difference for others produces the greatest personal satisfaction. At this point, he was determined to figure out how he could earn a comfortable living while making a difference for others.

In 1980, Ray Dirks founded a new daily newspaper, the *Wall Street Final*. It sought to capitalize on a technological breakthrough that allowed a newspaper containing closing stock market prices to be sold at Grand Central Station in New York City each day by 5:00 P.M. The late Priscilla Meyer, formerly of the *Wall Street Journal* and *Forbes*, edited the newspaper, and she hired Charles to be its daily stock market columnist. Before the *Wall Street Final* had worked out all of its start-up issues, however, both the *New York Daily News* and the *New York Post* came out with closing stock market price editions. As a result, the *Wall Street Final* lasted for only six months. Soon after it ceased publication, both the *New York Daily News* and the *New York Post* shut down their closing price editions.

In 1982, Charles moved to Seaside Park, New Jersey. Within a year, he bought control of various undeveloped parcels in Ocean County, New Jersey, which is located 60 miles from the Lincoln Tunnel entrance to New York City. Real estate development in Ocean County had stopped dead during the energy crisis that began in 1973, but Charles saw opportunity there because he believed oil prices and mortgage interest rates would eventually tumble. As early as 1980 in the *Wall Street Final*, Charles had predicted that crude oil prices were bound to decline. With crude oil at $40 per barrel, energy costs were accounting for 10 percent of U.S. national income, a situation that could not continue indefinitely. For comparison, crude oil prices at $40 to $50 per barrel today are equal to about 3 percent or 5 percent of U.S. national income. In 1983, mortgage interest rates plunged from nearly 20 percent to 11 percent, and the outer suburbs of American cities became viable for development.

By 1988, Charles controlled various properties in Ocean County with mortgages of between $15 million and $20 million. After the October 1987 stock market crash, however, the real estate market turned cold, and almost nothing sold. Charles' biggest lender, Citifederal Savings and Loan, eventually went bust. After the government took it over, all of Charles' loans were called. No partial payments were permitted, even though Charles believed that if he were given the time and the opportunity, he would have been able to sell everything off piecemeal, repay the bank debt, and still have several million dollars left over. Now he faced a grim situation: He could come up with several million dollars in cash—when no other banks were making new loans—or declare personal bankruptcy. Even though the individual properties he controlled were more valuable than the debt, he was forced to liquidate all of his assets and declare personal bankruptcy in December 1989.

This experience taught Charles a crucial lesson about the distinction between value and price: Value is the intrinsic worth of an asset, while price is the amount of money that a buyer agrees to pay a seller for an asset. He also learned that asset prices are determined primarily by liquidity (the supply of an asset and the amount of cash available to buy it) rather than value (the amount of income the asset generates). This simple distinction was the foundation not only for Charles' next move but for a new investment paradigm: liquidity theory.

THE FOUNDING OF TRIMTABS

In 1990, Charles decided to make a fresh start, and he founded Market TrimTabs in Santa Rosa, California. By that time, fax machines were widely used on Wall Street, so Charles could do stock market research from the wine country of northern California and transmit it to clients before the market opened each day. TrimTabs' first client was Meyer Berman, who for the second time in Charles' life provided what he needed to move forward. Thank you, Meyer! TrimTabs' first recommendation was the short sale of Midlantic National Bank, which traded in the high $20s in January 1990. Ultimately Midlantic was taken over at a price of under $10 to save the bank from bankruptcy.

In its early years, TrimTabs focused on providing stock ideas primarily to hedge funds. The only model Charles had for a successful weekly stock market column was the "Up and Down Wall Street" column written by Alan Abelson, his former boss and mentor. Charles analyzed the overall stock market—as Abelson still does—before delving into the details of why to short or buy particular stocks. In analyzing the overall stock market, Charles discovered that no one was tracking money flows into and out of the stock market on a regular basis. Granted, the Federal Reserve, Salomon Brothers, and Goldman Sachs used U.S. government data to analyze these flows on a quarterly basis. But instead of relying on government data—just like sausage, no one should watch how government data is made—Charles began searching for real-time data on money flows of all sorts, including corporate buying and selling, mutual funds flow, and margin debt.

As 1994 ended, corporate America became a heavy net buyer of equities, and in 1995 inflows into stock mutual funds from individuals began to accelerate. At the same time, Charles realized that short selling—TrimTabs' specialty—was not working well unless a "smoking gun" was uncovered because of the sheer volume of cash flooding into the stock market from corporate America and individual investors. In August 1995—nine months into a five-year bull market—he began *Liquidity TrimTabs*, a weekly publication analyzing stock market liquidity. Over the next five years, he developed liquidity theory to the point where he felt he had mastered the basics. As the firm developed into the only independent research service that publishes detailed daily coverage of stock market liquidity, including daily mutual funds flow and withheld income and employment tax collections, it became known as TrimTabs Investment Research. The firm concentrated on selling daily and weekly liquidity research to the major financial players in the U.S. stock market. TrimTabs currently offers two products for individual investors. First, *TrimTabs Monthly Liquidity* provides individual investors with a monthly digest of TrimTabs liquidity, personal income, and employment research. Second, as we write this book, we are in the process of launching the TrimTabs Model Portfolio Fund. This mutual fund, which will be available to individual investors only via a prospectus, will mimic the TrimTabs model portfolio. We are also working with a money management firm to allow investors to create portfolios that either mimic or are more aggressive than the TrimTabs model portfolio. For the latest information on these new products, please visit www.trimtabs.com.

SOME LESSONS OF LIFE

At TrimTabs, we are always trying to exceed our clients' expectations, so here are the answers to the questions Charles is most frequently asked about living life.

The Secret of Happiness

The secret of happiness is simple: want what you've got. If you want to be unhappy, want what you haven't got. If you want to be extremely unhappy, desperately want what you haven't got.

We do not mean to suggest that no one should strive for goals. But you can be happy while striving for a goal only if you truly want to be striving for that goal.

How to Live a Satisfying Life

The secret to living a satisfying life is making your life be about others. If you want to take a "life sucks and then you die" approach to your life, make your life about you: your needs, your desires, your fantasies. If you want your life to be extremely satisfying, make it about the needs, desires, and fantasies of the people in your life.

The Secret of Success

Charles has built a multimillion-dollar net worth three times from nothing, so he feels he has some useful points to share about becoming successful.

The secret of success is giving 100 percent without stopping, never quitting no matter how many rejections you get. A year before Naomi and Wynonna Judd moved in with Charles in 1979, Josipa Lisaz, the leading Yugoslavian chanteuse at the time, was Charles' houseguest. Lisaz was a far more talented singer than Naomi Judd, but she never gave 100 percent. She always held back and assumed that sheer talent would make her as successful in the United States as she was back home. It never did. By contrast, for five years, Naomi Judd did everything possible, within her own unique code of ethics, for her and her daughter to become successful. She obviously succeeded.

Dr. Henry Jarecki, the head of Mocatta Metals when it was the largest gold and silver trading company in the world and currently the chairman of Falconwood Trading, is another example of how persistence is the key to success. Jarecki claims he was lucky to get into the silver trading business while practicing psychiatry in New Haven, Connecticut. In the late 1960s, no fewer than 12 banks rejected his scheme to make a profit while paying a higher price than anyone else for demonetized silver certificates. He says he was lucky that the thirteenth bank he approached agreed to fund his plan. In our opinion, Jarecki was not lucky—he was successful. He did not let rejections from a dozen banks prevent him from reaching his goal.

Success and failure are neither good nor bad. Success or failure is only possible when you strive for something 100 percent. Sports are so important because they are about playing all out for no real reason. Indeed, true failure is never giving 100 percent for anything. Without striving 100 percent for a goal, nothing new is possible. Even winning the lottery becomes a losing proposition.

To summarize, wanting a life of playing full out all the time to make a difference for others creates a happy, satisfying, and successful life. Now that we have revealed some of the secrets of life, the next two chapters introduce the principles of liquidity theory, which Charles has refined over the past 11 years.

CHAPTER 3

The Principles of Liquidity Theory

Most traders lose money in the stock market. The five months from November 1999 to March 2000 immediately preceded the top of the biggest stock market bubble in history. During these five months, investors pumped $270 billion into the market. Of this total, $135 billion flowed into stock mutual funds and another $135 billion flowed directly into stocks such as Cisco Systems, JDS Uniphase, and Sun Microsystems—stocks that dropped more than 80 percent during the two years following the top. While the most aggressive Nasdaq stocks peaked in March and April, the rest of the market did not top out until August. Between April and August, $200 billion poured into stocks: about $100 billion into stock mutual funds and another $100 billion in direct investments. The total inflow of $470 billion between November 1999 and August 2000 does not even include the $150 billion in foreign money that found its way into U.S. stocks. The bottom line: Investors dumped at least half a trillion dollars into the U.S. stock market between November 1999 and August 2000. The ensuing bear market would take the S&P 500 and the Nasdaq as much as 50 percent and 78 percent, respectively, below their record highs.

By the time the market bottomed in October 2002, at least $300 billion of the $500 billion pumped into the market at the top was lost. While it is not much consolation, individuals were not alone in their losses. Brokerage firms also did a fine job of losing money at the top. On August 30, 2000—two days before the S&P 500 topped out at 1,530.01—Credit Suisse First Boston announced it would purchase brokerage firm Donaldson Lufkin & Jenrette for $13.6 billion, mostly in cash.

"Buy high and sell low" is the motto of most individual investors. At least that is what their actions suggest. Many of the same investors who pumped at least half a trillion dollars into the stock market at the top sold right at the bottom. From June 2002 through February 2003, individuals cashed in more than $100 billion in stock mutual fund shares at prices 50 percent to 75 percent below what they paid for them. This $100 billion in redemptions cost investors more than $200 billion to buy. And these figures just include mutual funds. Individuals probably lost even more in direct holdings of stocks, some of which crashed straight down to zero.

Yet followers of liquidity theory would not have lost money. They also would have known there was one consistent seller at the top—corporate America. In November 1999, public companies and the insiders who run them became heavy sellers. They continued selling through July 2002—when they suddenly turned very bullish. In other words, when individuals were pumping big bucks into the stock market, companies were sucking that money out. When individuals panicked and dumped their shares at the bottom, companies were ready and willing to buy the stocks they were unloading at dirt cheap prices. With whom would you rather invest: corporate America or the suckers?

Millions of unwitting investors suffered trillions in losses during the 2000–2002 bear market by adopting a do-it-yourself approach to managing their money. At the height of the dot-com bubble in 2000, many investors barely understood the companies whose shares they were buying, let alone the finer points of stock market investing. Yet as we explain in Chapter 1, anyone capable of accumulating large sums of cash—even through inheritance—is capable of managing his or her own assets. Stripping away all of the hype of the financial media, it is not difficult to understand the basic principles on which the stock market operates. This chapter introduces the fundamentals of liquidity theory and explains how it works to predict the direction of the stock market.

THE STOCK MARKET CASINO

Every institution has a design purpose, but often it is not what most people think. Many individual investors hope the stock market will be their personal stairway to financial heaven, showering them with comfortable retirements, exciting vacations, and educations for their children at leading universities. Stockbrokers hope to profit from every trade, whether their clients are buying or selling new or existing shares of stock. Money managers hope the stocks in their portfolios continue to rise so their incomes— usually a percentage of assets under management—rise along with them.

Yet the design purpose of the stock market is none of these things. According to the Securities Industry Association, the design purpose of the stock market is to provide funding for industry. We agree wholeheartedly with this statement, but we need to consider it more carefully. Where does industry obtain the money it needs? It obtains it from investors. The design purpose of the stock market is to separate investors continually from their cash while leaving them with smiles on their faces so they return for more. If this design purpose sounds familiar, that is because it is. It is exactly the same as the design purpose of a casino.

While the stock market casino is not always as flashy as the attractions of the Las Vegas Strip, its rewards can be far greater for those who understand how it operates. The house in the stock market casino consists of public companies and the insiders—chief executive officers, presidents, vice presidents, officers, and directors—who run them. The players in the stock market casino consist of investors—hedge funds, pension funds, mutual funds, and individual investors. Two things change hands between the house and the players: shares of stock and money.

How do public companies (the house) make money? The answer is simple. Public companies (the house) sell shares of stock to investors (the players) in exchange for money. As an investor, when you buy a share of stock in a public company, what you are really buying is a stake in the ownership of that company. Suppose you purchase one share of Starbucks stock, and suppose Starbucks has issued 400 million shares of its stock. With your single share of Starbucks stock, you become an owner of Starbucks. Granted, you own only one-400,000,000th of Starbucks, but you become a fractional owner nonetheless. Mutual funds that invest in stocks work much the same way. If you purchase a single share of the Vanguard 500 Index Fund (VFINX), you are buying a fractional share in all of the 500 companies this index fund owns. Whether directly or through mutual funds, investors (the players) buy shares from public companies (the house) hoping the shares of stock they are buying will be worth more in the future than the amount of money they are paying for them in the present. At the same time, public companies (the house) may choose to buy shares of stock from investors (the players) in exchange for money. Why would public companies buy back their own shares? They would do so if they believed that the current price was cheap compared to what their company was really worth.

Every prospective investor in the stock market casino must understand that the stock market casino exists to make money for the house. It does not exist to make money for the players. This is not to say players cannot make money in the stock market casino. In fact, the primary purpose of this book is to show you how to make money in the stock market. Yet prospective investors must always bear in mind that the stock market casino is designed for the benefit of public companies (the house), not for the benefit of investors (the players).

So far we have surveyed the components of the stock market casino.

We have learned the stock market casino exists to raise capital for public companies (the house), which buy and sell shares of stock to investors (the players) in exchange for money. But what determines the price of the shares in the stock market casino? How do the house and the players determine the prices at which they will buy and sell shares? The answer: supply and demand. The stock market casino is a market just like any other market, and the supply of shares and the demand for them are the primary determinants of stock prices.

SUPPLY AND DEMAND IN ACTION: ORANGES

To get an idea of how supply and demand affect the price of a good in a market, let's step away from the stock market casino and consider an example everyone can readily understand: oranges. If you are already familiar with how supply and demand operate in a market, you can skip this discussion and continue reading after the four figures.

As first-year university students learn in Economics 101, the price of a good, such as oranges, is a function of both the supply of oranges and the demand for oranges. We plot supply and demand graphically, as shown in Figure 3.1.

The upward-sloping solid line represents the supply of oranges, while the downward-sloping dashed line represents the demand for oranges. These lines reflect common sense. As the price of oranges (horizontal axis) increases, the supply of oranges rises, as suppliers are willing to produce

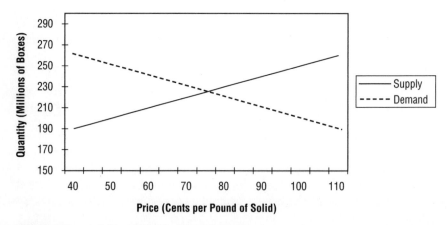

FIGURE 3.1   Supply and Demand for Oranges

more oranges at higher prices. At the same time, the demand for oranges falls, as consumers are willing to buy fewer oranges as the price of oranges rises. The point at which the supply line and the demand line intersect is the market price of oranges. At this point, the supply of oranges and the demand for oranges is balanced.

We can show visually how the market price of oranges responds to changes in supply and demand. Suppose the demand for oranges plummets because more people are limiting their intake of carbohydrates and are drinking less orange juice. We show this change graphically in Figure 3.2. The dashed line represents the lower demand for oranges. Note that the market price (intersection of supply and new demand) of oranges has now declined substantially, as one would expect when supply holds steady and demand plummets. If demand for oranges had increased for some reason, the market price of oranges would have risen.

Changes in supply can also affect the market price of oranges. Suppose a severe frost hits Florida, wiping out nearly all of the state's citrus crop. Since Florida accounts for a substantial percentage of America's orange production, the supply of oranges would obviously plummet. We show this change graphically in Figure 3.3. The upward-sloping dashed line represents the lower supply of oranges. Note that the market price of oranges (intersection of demand and new supply) has now risen substantially, as one would expect when supply declines and demand holds steady. Similarly, if the supply of oranges had increased for some reason, the market price of oranges would have declined.

When the supply of oranges increases and the demand for oranges decreases, or vice versa, the effect on the price of oranges is even more

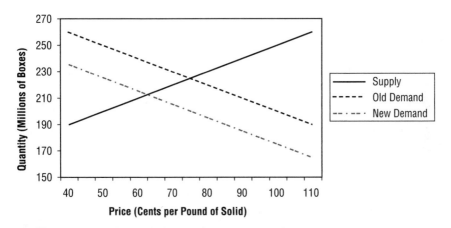

FIGURE 3.2 Decrease in Demand for Oranges

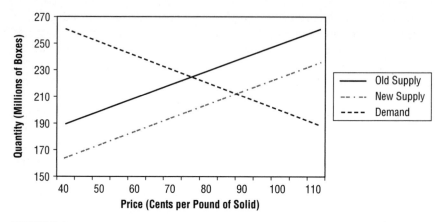

FIGURE 3.3 Decrease in Supply of Oranges

significant. Suppose that just as low-carb diets fall out of favor and people are drinking more orange juice, a severe frost hits Florida, hurting the orange harvest. We show this change graphically in Figure 3.4. The dashed lines represent the lower supply and the higher demand for oranges. Note that the market price of oranges (intersection of new demand and new supply) has now risen dramatically, as one would expect when supply declines and demand increases.

This example is deceptively simple because we assigned values to supply and demand arbitrarily. Projecting the precise impact of supply and de-

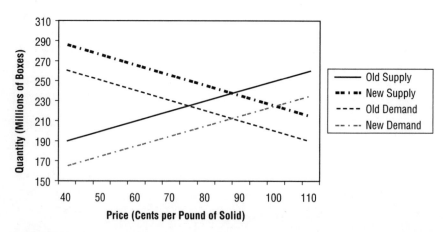

FIGURE 3.4 Decrease in Supply of Oranges and Increase in Demand for Oranges

mand changes on the price of a good is not easy. In the case of oranges, the supply of oranges can change based on many exogenous factors: the number of orange growers, the climate in orange-producing areas, the prices of inputs like labor and machinery required to produce oranges, technological changes in orange production, and government regulations. Demand for oranges is equally responsive to changes in many factors: the number of orange consumers, consumer preferences, and the price of orange substitutes like grapefruit. Forecasting changes in supply and demand, even for a relatively simple commodity like oranges, is challenging. For more complex products—such as plasma televisions, trucks, or machine tools—the task becomes even more difficult.

What we have tried to convey in this example is that the price of a good in a market depends on the supply of the good and the demand for the good. Note that the market price of oranges did not depend on the intrinsic value of the oranges. The market price of oranges did not decline in Figure 3.2 or rise in Figure 3.3 because of any changes in the taste or nutritional value of oranges. In both cases, the fundamental value of the good—oranges—was exactly the same as it was before the shifts in supply and demand in the market. Thus, the fundamental value of oranges and the price of oranges are different.

To add a bit of complexity to the interaction of supply and demand, let's consider the use of leverage to purchase a home. Suppose a fixer-upper in Beverly Hills, California, currently sells for $2 million. Clearly this home has fundamental value: value as shelter from the elements, value as a place for a couple to raise a family, value as a status symbol. Yet the price of this home may fluctuate wildly in the marketplace in any given year. During a year of economic expansion, its price might rise 15 percent. By contrast, during a recession year, its price might fall 10 percent. Through all of the ups and downs of the single-family housing market, however, the fundamental value of the home as a place to live and raise a family would not change. All else being equal, it would still retain just as much of its fundamental value—a shelter from the elements, a place for a couple to raise a family, and a status symbol—throughout the entire period.

Let's assume no borrowing capability exists in the real estate market and a buyer of this home is required to pay all cash for it. Would its price still be $2 million or even 10 percent to 20 percent less? Of course not. Its price would plummet if no money were available for mortgages. By contrast, let's assume a buyer could purchase it for only $50,000—2.5 percent down—and carry the balance on an interest-only mortgage at a 1 percent interest rate. Thus, the monthly mortgage payments for this lovely $2 million fixer-upper would be about $1,625. Would home prices under these conditions soar to ridiculous levels? Of course they would. Yet the value of this home would never change. Rather, the price of the home would change, along with the impact of the changing price on the home-owner's lifestyle.

Incidentally, investors were permitted to buy stock on 90 percent margin during the 1920s stock market bubble. To buy $1,000 worth of RCA—the Cisco of its day—investors only had to put up $100. If RCA doubled, investors would make 10 times their investment. Of course, if RCA declined just 10 percent, investors would be wiped out. Despite all of the mythology, what really caused the Great Depression was not the stock market crash. The Great Depression was precipitated by the ac-tions of politicians, which wiped out a large percentage of U.S. banks and their depositors. Granted, the stock market crash weakened many a bank's balance sheet, but if today's regulations protecting depositors had been in effect in the 1920s, the Great Depression would never have occurred.

PLAYING ON THE SIDE OF THE HOUSE

To win in the stock market casino, you must know not only the design of the game but the role of Wall Street brokerage firms and the two main stock market paradigms. Most investors mistakenly believe that brokers and analysts who work for Wall Street brokerage firms are on their side. These people are in the game to make money for themselves by convincing suckers, otherwise known as the public, to invest in their most lucrative products: new offerings. Brokerage firms are paid for stock trades on a commission basis, but all stock trades are not equal. These days, individual investors can buy lots of stock online for no more than a $20 commission. Institutional brokerage firms now charge a commission of about 3 cents per share for a trade. On a $50 stock, this commission amounts to 0.06 percent. Yet when suckers buy newly printed shares, brokerage firms re-ceive a commission of between 3 percent and 7 percent, which means a new offering priced at $50 per share yields between $1.50 to $3.50 per share as a commission.

Brokerage firms make much more money selling new shares to suckers than they do trading existing shares, and they earn nearly nothing from in-vestors who dollar-cost average into index mutual funds directly with mu-tual fund companies. That is why you almost never see a brokerage firm predict that the stock market will decline. Brokerage firms do not care whether the stock market rises or falls. All they care about is whether you buy new offerings from them. Do you see now why Wall Street is a casino designed to get you to play and lose your money? Meanwhile, who pays for the lavish year-end bonuses, expense accounts, and corporate jets at Wall Street brokerage firms? If you invest with these firms, you do! You pay for them just as surely as you pay for all of the supposed flash and trash at the gaudiest casinos.

Two main stock market paradigms dominate the investment world. The most popular paradigm, which is often termed value investing or fundamental analysis, holds that stock prices are driven by the expected future earnings of public companies. When earnings rise, stock prices rise; when earnings fall, stock prices fall. Remember, the U.S. economy has grown faster than any other economy in the history of the world. Even the economy of the Roman Empire at its height and the economy of the British Empire during the eighteenth and nineteenth centuries did not grow as fast as the U.S. economy has over the past 200 years. Since value investors argue that stock prices are a function of earnings and earnings growth is likely to match the growth of the U.S. economy, it is no surprise brokers always advise investors, "Buy now!" Fundamental analysis serves the same purpose as a barker in front of a con game who tries to separate suckers from their money. It performs the same function as casino advertising, which claims casinos are about winning—the casino winning, not you!

Technical analysis, which is embraced by a far smaller percentage of investment professionals, holds that future stock prices can be discerned by analyzing the movement of stock prices in the past. Technicians often use stock charts and various statistical indicators to determine when to buy and sell. Part Two shows why fundamental analysis and technical analysis are flawed and why liquidity—which measures the supply of stocks and the money available to buy them—is the primary determinant of stock prices.

So far we have learned that the stock market is basically a casino in which public companies (the house) and investors (the players) exchange shares of stock for money. We have also learned that the prices at which these shares of stock trade are determined by supply and demand. Now you may be asking, "All of this discussion is fine, but how do I actually make money in the stock market?" The answer is to use liquidity theory to play the stock market casino on the side of the house.

Regardless of your income or wealth, using liquidity theory to invest on the side of the house produces superior returns for two main reasons. First, public companies and the insiders who run them are the smartest investors in the stock market. They know more about their own business prospects and the outlook for the overall economy than anyone else, including highly paid Wall Street analysts and economists. After all, public companies and their leaders do business every day, and their collective actions in the stock market are one of the best leading indicators of the economy's growth prospects. Second, just like a Las Vegas casino, the stock market is rigged in favor of the house. As the house, public companies control the number of shares in the casino at any one time. When stock prices are high, they can sell a nearly infinite number of new shares to eager investors. When stock prices are low, they can buy back shares from investors that enhance the value of insiders' stock options. With inside knowledge of their own prospects, public companies are in an excellent position to know exactly when stock prices are unreasonably high and when they are unreasonably low.

This control over the number of available shares is particularly useful at market turning points. During a stock market bubble, investors practically clamor to buy stocks. At the same time as individuals and foreigners were pumping over $500 billion into U.S. stocks between November 1999 and August 2000, public companies and the insiders who run them were net sellers of $150 billion of new shares, net of cash takeovers and stock buybacks. Between June 2002 and March 2003, while individuals were heavy net sellers, public companies were net buyers of more than $50 billion of their own shares.

Public companies are perfectly willing to exchange shares of stock for cash during bubbles, since they know that once a bubble bursts, the cash they received for the new shares they sold will be far more valuable than the shares themselves. The opposite occurs during a bear market, when investors can hardly stand to even glance at their mutual fund and brokerage account statements. In the depths of a bear market, most investors want nothing more than to sell their stocks and retreat to the perceived safety of bonds and cash. Of course, public companies are more than willing to oblige them. Instead of selling new shares, as they would during a bubble, they buy back shares from investors at bargain prices, knowing the shares will be far more valuable than the cash they paid for them once the bear market ends.

Do you notice a pattern here? Public companies and investors act in completely different ways when faced with the same market circumstances. While public companies (the house) buy low and sell high, investors (the players) buy high and sell low. Is it any wonder that the house makes far more money than the players in the stock market casino?

The overwhelming majority of investors do not invest on the side of the house. Instead of watching what the house is doing and investing accordingly, they troll the popular press for the latest hot mutual funds and eagerly trade the changes to the recommended lists of their brokerage firms. Unfortunately, the overwhelming majority of investors also underperform the major stock market averages. Liquidity theory offers a better way to invest. The following chapter shows how it works.

CHAPTER 4

The Building Blocks of Liquidity Analysis

Deep in the bowels of an ocean-going ship, such as an aircraft carrier or a cruise liner, lies a trim tab. The trim tab is a minuscule rudder that runs the length of the main rudder. To change the ship's direction, one must first turn the trim tab, and then the main rudder follows. Even though the ship may weigh thousands of tons, any change in its direction begins with the movement of the small trim tab.

Just as the movement of a trim tab determines the direction of a ship, the trim tabs of liquidity theory are the key to understanding the direction of the stock market. In the stock market casino, liquidity is the relationship between the issuance and redemption of shares available for trading (float) and the amount of cash available for stock investment (flow). By tracking three liquidity trim tabs that measure the float and the flow, we can gauge where the stock market is likely to turn in the future. The first and most important of these trim tabs is the net change in the trading float of shares (L1), which measures the float. The next two trim tabs are U.S. equity mutual fund flows (L2) and margin debt (L3), which measure the flow. You need not have a mathematics or finance background to understand how these liquidity trim tabs work. All you need to know is some simple arithmetic. In the chapters in Part Two, we will provide more details on how to track and analyze each of the trim tabs described here.

CHANGE IN THE NET TRADING FLOAT OF SHARES (L1)

As discussed in the previous chapter, the participants in the stock market casino are public companies and the insiders who run them (the house) and investors (the players). The house and the players trade shares of stock for money. The market capitalization is the value of all of the shares of stock in the stock market casino, which is calculated by multiplying the most recent share price of all publicly traded companies by the number of shares outstanding. Stocks traded on the New York Stock Exchange (NYSE) comprise about 80 percent of the market capitalization, while stocks traded on the Nasdaq Stock Market comprise about 20 percent of the market capitalization. On September 30, 2004, the U.S. stock market had a market capitalization of $15.7 trillion. Liquidity theory is designed to predict the overall change in the market capitalization. In other words, it indicates whether the house is betting that the market capitalization will rise or fall. Liquidity theory is not concerned with the merits of individual stocks or sectors.

The most important liquidity measure is our first trim tab, the net change in the trading float of shares, which we call L1. L1 measures whether the house in the stock market casino is a net buyer or a net seller of stock. If L1 is positive, it means the trading float of shares is increasing and the house is a net seller of stock. If L1 is negative, it means the trading float of shares is shrinking and the house is a net buyer of stock. We are extremely interested to know whether the house is buying or selling. Over the more than 10 years we have tracked stock market liquidity, we have found L1 is the best leading indicator of the direction of the stock market.

We calculate L1 using four components:

1. *New stock buybacks.* A new stock buyback occurs when a public company buys back its shares from existing investors, usually in the open market. For example, Microsoft had 10.8 billion shares outstanding as of January 31, 2004, after it had repurchased $3.8 billion worth of its shares in 2003. By buying back these shares, Microsoft reduced the number of its shares outstanding. Companies generating free cash flow, which is defined as after-tax earnings plus noncash charges minus capital expenditures, generally use some of their free cash flow to buy back their shares, which increases the value of their shares they do not buy back. Stock buybacks are bullish for stock market liquidity because they reduce the supply of stock outstanding. Remember, if the supply of a stock declines—all else being equal—the price of that stock increases, since the same amount of money is chasing a smaller number of shares. Yet stock buybacks are not always what they seem. Although Microsoft bought back $3.8 billion worth of its shares in 2003, the number of Microsoft shares outstanding actually rose by 93.7 million shares in 2003. Since Microsoft shares traded for an average of about $25 per share in 2003, the trading float of Microsoft rose by about $2.3 billion in 2003 (93.7 million shares × $25 per share = $2.3 billion). This increase occurred even though Microsoft bought

back $3.8 billion in shares because Microsoft insiders sold $6.1 billion in shares that did not exist at the beginning of 2003 ($6.1 billion – $3.8 billion = $2.3 billion). These additional shares materialized due to exercises of stock options. Even though Microsoft made substantial re-purchases, the stock options sold by Microsoft insiders more than off-set the liquidity benefit of the buybacks. The same thing could happen with the massive $30 billion stock buyback Microsoft announced in July 2004. Exercises of stock options could easily offset the liquidity impact of this buyback.

2. *New cash takeovers.* Like new stock buybacks, new cash takeovers are bullish for stock market liquidity because they reduce the supply of shares outstanding. A new cash takeover occurs when a buyer—a pub-lic company, a private company, or a private investor—pays cash to take over a public company. For example, Cingular offered $41 billion in cash to take over AT&T Wireless in February 2004. When this deal was completed in November 2004, Cingular bought all of AT&T Wireless' shares from existing shareholders, removing them from the stock market casino. All else being equal, a lower supply of stock means higher stock prices.

3. *New offerings.* Unlike new stock buybacks and new cash takeovers, new offerings are bearish for stock market liquidity because they in-crease the supply of shares in the stock market casino. A new offering is a sale by a public company of additional shares of its stock. For ex-ample, General Electric sold a $3.8 billion secondary offering on March 8, 2004. Since General Electric shares traded for about $32 per share at that time, this deal increased the trading float of General Elec-tric shares by about 118.8 million shares ($3.8 billion ÷ $32 per share = 118.8 million shares). Other types of new offerings include initial public offerings, convertible bond offerings, and convertible preferred stock offerings. The distinctions between various types of new offer-ings will be covered in Part Two. For the moment, however, what is important to understand about new offerings is that they are bearish for stock market liquidity. All else being equal, a larger supply of shares means lower stock prices, since the same amount of money is chasing more shares.

4. *Insider selling.* The final component of L1 is insider selling. Insider selling occurs when corporate insiders—including top executives, board members, and major shareholders—sell shares in their company they own personally. For example, if a board member of Procter & Gamble sells shares she owns in her personal account, or if the CEO of Procter & Gamble sells some of his stock options that have unlocked, insider selling has occurred. Insider selling differs from new offerings

in one major respect. Insider selling involves individuals selling usually previously unregistered shares, while new offerings are sold by public companies themselves. Nevertheless, the effect of insider selling is the same as the effect of new offerings, since shares become available in the stock market casino that were not available before insiders sold them. Since insider selling increases the number of shares outstanding, it is bearish for liquidity, since a greater supply of shares means lower stock prices, all else being equal.

Using these four components, we can calculate L1:

$$\text{L1} = \text{New Offerings} + \text{Insider Selling} - \text{New Stock Buybacks}$$
$$- \tfrac{2}{3}\ \text{New Cash Takeovers} - \tfrac{1}{3}\ \text{Completed Cash Takeovers}$$

Remember, L1 measures whether the house is a net buyer or a net seller in the stock market casino. Positive L1 is bearish, since it means the house is selling more shares through new offerings and insider selling than it is buying through stock buybacks and cash takeovers. Negative L1 is bullish, since it means the house is buying more shares through stock buybacks and cash takeovers than it is selling through new offerings and insider selling. L1 allows investors to determine how the house is investing so they can play the stock market casino on the house's side of the table.

At this point, we should clarify two details of our L1 formula. First, we count the dollar amount of newly announced stock buybacks in our L1 formula when they are announced even though public companies do not repurchase their shares immediately after they announce a stock buyback. Instead, they typically buy back their shares over a period of 12 to 24 months. Unfortunately there is no way to track actual stock buybacks except through the quarterly and annual reports public companies are required to file with the U.S. Securities and Exchange Commission, and these reports are not available until months after the actual stock buybacks are completed. As Part Two discusses, we estimate actual stock buybacks in our short-term liquidity forecasts, but we use only new stock buybacks in our L1 formula.

Second, we include two-thirds of the dollar amount of a cash takeover in our L1 formula when it is announced and one-third of the dollar amount when it is completed. When a cash takeover is announced, arbitrageurs typically buy two-thirds of the stock of the target company within a week of the deal's announcement. They do so because they hope to profit from the difference in the price between the current value of the target company's stock and the value the acquiring company has offered to pay for the target company's stock. In purchasing the target company's stock, arbitrageurs take a calculated risk that the takeover will actually occur. Obviously such trades can be risky, but the rewards can also be handsome. In any case, we count only two-thirds of the dollar amount of a cash takeover immediately because that is roughly the proportion immediately removed from the hands of the public. We count the remaining one-third of the dollar amount of a cash takeover when the deal is completed.

L1 is determined entirely by the actions of the house in the stock market casino. The players have no direct control over it. Of course, the house can always buy more shares or sell more shares in response to what the players are doing, but the players themselves cannot directly control L1. The ability to control the number of shares in the stock market casino is what offers the house its advantage.

L1 is the best leading indicator of the future direction of the stock market. A negative L1 reading indicates the house is a net buyer of stocks, which suggests the stock market is likely to rise. Conversely, a positive L1 reading indicates the house is a net seller of stocks, which suggests the stock market is likely to fall. As we will see, L1 is not a guaranteed predictor of the future direction of the stock market. Other factors—most notably exogenous shocks and market psychology—can impact the stock market in ways L1 cannot predict. What liquidity analysis can offer, however, is the opportunity to place the odds in the stock market casino in your favor by investing on the side of the smart money—public companies and the insiders who run them.

U.S. EQUITY MUTUAL FUND FLOWS (L2)

The second major liquidity measure is U.S. equity mutual fund flows, which we call L2. While L1 indicates what the house is doing in the stock market casino, L2 indicates what the players are doing. We calculate L2 by totaling the amount of cash investors are either investing or withdrawing from mutual funds that invest in U.S. stocks.

While L2 is easier to calculate than L1, interpreting it is somewhat more difficult. At first, it may seem as if strong inflows into U.S. equity funds should be bullish for the stock market, while strong outflows should be bearish. After all, if demand for stocks is rising, stock prices should rise, all else being equal. Conversely, if demand for stocks is falling, stock prices should fall, all else being equal. Analyzing U.S. equity fund flows, however, is not quite so straightforward. Remember, L2 measures what the players are doing. The players are the dumb money in the stock market casino. They invariably buy high and sell low because they chase investments that have performed well in the recent past and shun investments that have performed poorly in the recent past. Thus, L2 is typically a lagging indicator, revealing more about what has happened than what will happen.

Why would we pay any attention to L2 if it typically tells us little about what will happen in the future? We do so because L2 is particularly useful in confirming market turning points. In abnormal markets—such as during bubbles or bottoms—L2 is a contrary indicator that often suggests when the market is likely to change direction. For example, March 2000 proved to be the top of the technology bubble. Investors were pouring money into U.S equity funds around this time: $31.4 billion in January 2000, $36.5 billion in February 2000, $33.4 billion in March 2000, and $30.8 billion in April 2000. Just as inflows peaked—February 2000 still holds the record for monthly U.S. equity fund inflows—the market cracked. Over the next 2.5 years, the Nasdaq lost more than 70 percent of its value, and the S&P 500 lost nearly 50 percent of its value. Unfortunately investors made sure they were fully invested immediately before the technology bubble burst. By contrast, U.S. equity funds usually see heavy outflows immediately before the market bottoms. For example, October 2002 and March 2003 marked the two bottoms of the most recent bear market. U.S. equity fund flows were negative immediately before each of these bottoms. U.S. equity funds had outflows for five straight months from June 2002 through October 2002 and for three straight months from December 2002 through February 2003. Investors usually rush for the exits immediately before the stock market recovers. Predicting when bubbles will burst and bottoms will form is one of the most difficult tasks for liquidity theory, but L2 is a contrary indicator that can help us make such predictions.

Of course, U.S. equity funds are not the only way to access the U.S. stock market. Investors can also choose to invest in U.S. stocks through exchange-traded funds (ETFs) and by purchasing U.S. stocks directly. Yet ETFs account for only a small fraction of total investment by individuals in the U.S. stock market, and direct investments in equities are not currently measurable. Thus, we use U.S. equity fund flows as a proxy for total investment in the stock market.

MARGIN DEBT (L3)

The third major liquidity measure is margin debt growth, which we call L3. L3 is the change in the amount of margin debt used to purchase stocks, as reported by the member firms of the NYSE. Margin debt is money an investor borrows from a brokerage firm at a fixed interest rate to buy securities. Here is how it works. Suppose an investor borrows $50,000 from Ameritrade at a 5 percent annualized interest rate. The investor uses the borrowed $50,000 to buy stocks. When the stocks are sold, the investor re-pays Ameritrade the borrowed amount of $50,000 as well as the interest expense, which would be $2,500 if the trade lasted for one year. The investor then pockets the profits or absorbs the loss from the stocks pur-chased with the borrowed $50,000. The investor obviously hopes the profit from the stocks he or she purchased exceeds the interest cost of the borrowed $50,000.

Margin debt is a form of leverage, which means investors can multiply the number of shares purchased for essentially the same amount of cash. Rapid growth in margin debt indicates investors are extraordinarily opti-mistic about the future prospects of the stock market. L3 rises most sharply after a prolonged period of strong stock market returns. Con-versely, L3 falls dramatically only after a prolonged period of poor stock market returns. Thus, L3 is even more of a lagging indicator than L2. Like L2, L3 is most useful as a contrary indicator in abnormal markets, such as during bubbles and at bottoms. For example, margin debt grew an aston-ishing $96.3 billion from the end of October 1999 through the end of March 2000, just before the technology bubble burst. This level of growth was more than three times higher than the previous annual record of $28.9 billion in 1997, making it a screaming sell signal. Not surprisingly, margin debt declined each year in 2000, 2001, and 2002 as the bubble burst and the stock market plunged. As the stock market recovered in 2003, investor optimism returned again. Margin debt surged $34.3 billion, a figure sec-ond only to the growth during 2000.

THE ANATOMY OF BULL AND BEAR MARKETS

So far we have learned about tracking the action in the stock market casino using L1 for the house and L2 and L3 for the players. But how do these in-dicators play out in practice? Part Three provides an extensive account of recent stock market history from a liquidity perspective, but here we will survey how L1, L2, and L3 typically interact.

At the beginning of a typical bull market, we would expect L1 to be strongly negative, since the house would be buying far more shares through cash takeovers and stock buybacks than it would be selling through new offerings and insider selling. At the same time, we would ex-pect L2 and L3 to be negative as well, since the players are typically selling stocks at the beginning of a bull market and are hardly interested in buying stocks on margin. As a bull market gathers strength, we would expect L1 to remain negative—the house would still be buying—but L2 would turn increasingly positive as investors react favorably to stock market gains. L3 might turn slightly positive as well as investors' appetite for risk increases. In the late stages of a bull market, we would expect L1 to turn increasingly positive as companies gradually become more interested in selling stock to enthusiastic players rather than buying other companies for cash or repurchasing shares at inflated prices. At the same time, we would expect L2 and L3 to become strongly positive as investors, noticing the recent gains, become more willing to risk money in the stock market.

During the height of a bubble, L1 usually turns strongly positive as companies sell as many shares as possible to eager players. Meanwhile, L2 and L3 explode as the players rush to buy as many shares as possible. According to liquidity theory, a bubble exists when the house is selling heavily—L1 is strongly positive—while the players are buying heavily—L2 and L3 are strongly positive. Since the house can sell an infinite number of new shares to eager players, a bubble pops when new offerings and insider selling overwhelm inflows.

A bear market usually begins with strongly positive L1, since the house is continuing to sell as many shares as possible to eager players. L2 turns increasingly negative as losses mount, and the players begin to realize the party is over. As the bear market grinds on, however, L1 turns increasingly negative as well. Not only is the house less willing and less able to unload new shares to increasingly disillusioned players, but lower stock prices make the house more inclined to buy shares than sell them. At the same time, L2 and L3 turn even more negative as the players sour on the stock market. According to liquidity theory, a bottom exists when the house is buying heavily—L1 is strongly negative—while the players are selling heavily—L2 and L3 are strongly negative. Once the house begins buying more than the players are selling, a new bull market is born, and the market cycle repeats itself. Of course, our liquidity indicators do not always interact in such neat patterns. Hopefully, however, this chapter has clarified the liquidity paradigm.

CONCLUSION

Liquidity theory is a powerful tool that enables you to invest on the side of the house in the stock market casino. By following the actions of the house and investing accordingly, you can achieve investment returns superior to those of the vast majority of professional investment managers.

You may have noticed that earnings are never discussed in this chapter. Liquidity theory ignores earnings trends because stock prices are primarily a function of stock market liquidity—the money available in the stock market casino to buy and sell shares of stock—rather than the fundamental value of stocks. The next chapter explains why following the cult of earnings that has developed on Wall Street offers investors little chance of outperforming the major stock market averages and why liquidity theory is a superior approach to stock market investing.

PART TWO

Inside Liquidity Theory

CHAPTER 5

Demolishing the Cult of Earnings

"**E**arnings, earnings, earnings" is the mantra of Wall Street. Price-earnings (P/E) ratios, earnings growth, consensus forward earnings—earnings dominate the discussion of the stock market in the financial media. The overwhelming majority of investment professionals believe the single most important determinant of a company's stock price is the future expected earnings of a company. As expected future earnings rise, stock prices rise; as expected future earnings fall, stock prices fall. This chapter explains why earnings do not drive stock prices despite the cultlike following they enjoy on Wall Street.

THE EARNINGS MYTH

Before we dismantle the cult of earnings, we need to explain what earnings are and how they are used in value investing. In general, earnings are defined as follows:

Earnings = Revenues − Cost of Sales − Operating Expenses − Taxes

Note that this definition is extremely general. As we discuss, financial analysts and accountants have developed numerous types of earnings, each with its own rules of which items to include and exclude in this formula.

Companies exist to produce earnings for shareholders. Value investors contend that earnings are the single most important determinant of a stock's price because they are the best indication of a company's expected future return. In other words, they claim that a stock's price rises when its expected future return rises and falls when its expected future return falls, assuming the state of the company's balance sheet is unchanged.

Here is a simple example of how value investing works in practice. Suppose Bob, a value investor, is analyzing Coca-Cola stock. How does he decide whether the stock is an attractive investment? First, Bob estimates how much per share he expects Coca-Cola to earn during the current year. He pegs this figure at $2 per share. Next, Bob considers the P/E ratio—otherwise known as the earnings multiple—of Coca-Cola stock. If Coca-Cola trades for $40 per share and he estimates that Coca-Cola will earn $2 per share during the current year, Coca-Cola is trading at a current P/E ratio of 20 ($40 ÷ $2 = 20). Bob believes Coca-Cola is fairly valued at this earnings multiple.

Suppose Coca-Cola unveils a new line of beverages. It proves so popular that Bob believes it will add $0.10 per share to Coca-Cola's earnings during the current year. Coca-Cola's other products are also experiencing much stronger than expected demand, and a major competitor is forced into Chapter 11 bankruptcy. Bob figures these developments will add $0.15 per share to Coca-Cola's earnings that year. Meanwhile, anticipating the impact of this good news, investors have bid up Coca-Cola to $42 per share. Is the stock still a good value? Given these new developments, Bob estimates the earnings per share of Coca-Cola during the current year will reach $2.25 ($2.00 + $0.10 + $0.15 = $2.25). He still believes 20 is a reasonable current P/E ratio for Coca-Cola, so he calculates the fair value of Coca-Cola at $45 per share ($2.25 × 20 = $45). As a result, he decides to buy more Coca-Cola shares. Assuming the earnings multiple remains unchanged, he believes Coca-Cola should command a higher stock price because its expected earnings for the current year have risen by $0.25 per share.

This example is oversimplified in a number of ways. First, nearly all value investors attempt to project future earnings beyond the current year. Second, value investors are most strongly attracted to companies with strong balance sheets and limited amounts of debt. Third, many factors other than the ones mentioned in this example—such as acquisitions, stock option grants, energy costs, and regulatory and tax changes—can affect a value investor's estimate of a company's expected future earnings. Fourth, a value investor may decide a stock ought to trade at a cheaper or a richer multiple of earnings due to company-specific issues, industry dynamics, macroeconomic trends, or social or political changes. We use the Coca-Cola example to illustrate the basic premise of value investing: stock prices are driven by expected future earnings. Tens of thousands of securities analysts, many with advanced degrees from prestigious universities, are paid handsomely to estimate the expected future earnings of public companies, market sectors, and the stock market as a whole. Investors pay hundreds of millions of dollars for access to fundamental analysis by major Wall Street brokerage firms and boutique investment houses. Most of this research rests on the premise that expected future earnings drive stock prices.

Nothing in this chapter is meant to denigrate the work of those security analysts who can pick the winners and short the losers in the stock market. Yet the success of these analysts in picking stocks has little to do with earnings, especially in the short run. Instead, it has a great deal to do with a thorough awareness of all of the liquidity and psychological phenomena that drive the pricing of stocks.

VALUE VERSUS PRICE

As we have indicated earlier in this book, the premise that earnings drive stock prices is simply wrong. If you are attempting to predict the direction of individual stocks or the stock market as a whole based on changes in expected future earnings, you are playing a losing game except at extremes. Remember the distinction between value and price discussed in earlier chapters? This distinction is the primary reason the cult of earnings has failed investors. When you invest based on earnings, you are investing based on value even though value is not what drives stock prices except in the very long run.

To clarify the distinction between value and price in the stock market, consider one of the darlings of the technology bubble: Cisco Systems. On March 27, 2000, Cisco stock closed at an all-time split-adjusted high of $80.06. On October 8, 2002, Cisco bottomed at $8.60—a loss of nearly 90 percent. From this bottom to the end of its fiscal year in July 2003, however, Cisco rose more than 130 percent to $19.49. Was value driving these price fluctuations? Figure 5.1 is revealing.

According to its 2003 annual report, Cisco reported net income of $0.29 per diluted share in fiscal 1999, which increased 24 percent to $0.36 per diluted share in fiscal 2000. Over the same period, however, Cisco's stock price jumped more than 100 percent! Clearly something other than earnings was at work. After reporting a loss of $0.14 per diluted share in fiscal 2001, Cisco's earnings recovered to $0.25 per diluted share in fiscal 2002 and $0.50 per diluted share in fiscal 2003. In other words, Cisco reported earnings per diluted share in fiscal 2003 that were 38 percent higher than those in fiscal 2000, when Cisco stock reached its all-time high. Yet at the end of fiscal 2003, Cisco stock traded 70 percent below where it traded at the end of fiscal 2000! Again, something other than earnings was driving Cisco's shares.

What changed? At the height of the technology mania, investors were willing to pay top dollar for technology darlings like Cisco. For instance, Cisco shares traded at a staggering 180 times fiscal 2000 earnings per diluted share at the end of fiscal 2000. After the technology bubble burst,

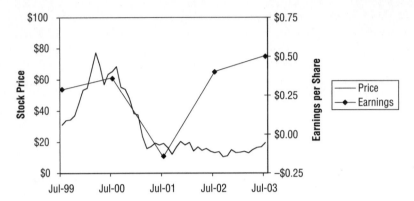

FIGURE 5.1   Cisco Stock Price versus Cisco Diluted Earnings per Share, July 1999
to July 2003
Raw data obtained from Yahoo! Finance, Cisco Systems.

many investors who held their Cisco shares through the plunge faced paper
losses of more than 75 percent. As a result, investors became far less willing to shower Cisco with cash. At the end of fiscal 2003, Cisco traded for
40 times fiscal 2003's earnings per diluted share. Accepting earnings per diluted share as a measure of value, Cisco shares held far more value at the
end of fiscal 2003 than they did at the end of fiscal 2000. Each Cisco share
earned $0.50 in fiscal 2003 instead of $0.36 in fiscal 2000. Yet value and
price are not the same! Even though Cisco shares had more value at the
end of fiscal 2003 than they did at the end of fiscal 2000, investors in 2003
were not willing to pay anywhere near what they had paid for them in
2000. Cisco's stock price over this period was not driven by value. Instead,
it was driven by the speculation of eager investors chasing one of the hot
stocks of the Internet revolution.

Lest anyone assume earnings and stock prices are unrelated only at
high-flying technology companies, consider a somewhat stodgier firm: Illinois Tool Works. (See Figure 5.2.)

In fiscal 1999, Illinois Tool Works earned $2.76 per diluted share. In
fiscal 2000, it earned $3.15 per diluted share, a respectable 14 percent in-
crease. Yet the price of Illinois Tool Works' stock fell 12 percent from the
end of fiscal 1999 to the end of fiscal 2000. The stock price declined not
because the company's earnings fell but because "old economy" companies—in other words, companies running real businesses generating real
profits—were out of favor among investors. A few years later, in fiscal
2003, Illinois Tool Works earned $3.32 per diluted share. While this figure
was only 5 percent higher than the $3.15 per diluted share it earned in

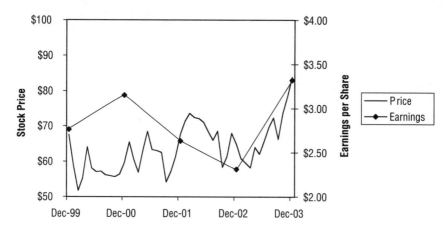

FIGURE 5.2 Illinois Tool Works Stock Price versus Illinois Tool Works Diluted Earnings per Share, December 1999 to December 2003
Raw data obtained from Yahoo! Finance, Illinois Tool Works.

fiscal 2000, Illinois Tool Works' stock traded 41 percent higher at the end of fiscal 2003 than it did at the end of fiscal 2000. Even over fairly lengthy periods, earnings do not drive stock prices.

Not only does attempting to invest based on trends in expected future earnings fail to work for individual stocks, but it also does not work for the stock market as a whole. Take a look at Figure 5.3, which plots the S&P 500 against consensus forward earnings for the S&P 500 from January 1995 through May 2004. Consensus forward earnings are the dollar amounts per share that analysts surveyed by Thomson Financial expect S&P 500 companies to earn during the next four quarters.

Do expected future earnings drive stock prices? At first glance, this graph might suggest they do. After all, the trends of both the S&P 500 and forward earnings rise, fall, and rise again. A more careful look at the graph reveals several problems. Perhaps the most obvious problem is that the S&P 500 was far more volatile than forward earnings. From 1995 to 2000, the S&P 500 rose far more rapidly than forward earnings, and from 2001 to 2003, the S&P 500 dropped far more rapidly than forward earnings. What about the predictive value of forward earnings? If earnings drive stock prices, then forward earnings should begin rising before upturns and begin falling before downturns. As the graph shows, however, this action did not occur. Consider the period from August 1998 through June 1999. Due to the Asian currency crisis and massive problems at Long-Term Capital Management, the S&P 500 closed at 957.28 at the end of August 1998. By the end of June 1999—just 10 months later—the S&P

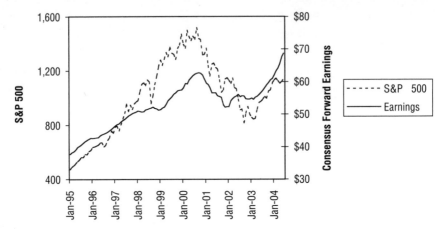

FIGURE 5.3 S&P 500 versus Consensus Forward Earnings for S&P 500, January 1995 to June 2004
Source: Yahoo! Finance, Thomson Financial.

500 rocketed to 1,372.71. Yet anyone hoping for a signal from earnings forecasts before investing missed the train big time. While the S&P 500 shot up 43 percent in 10 months, Table 5.1 shows what happened to forward earnings from the year before this surge to the year after it.

During the 12 months immediately preceding the rally, forward earnings barely budged, moving from $49.45 in August 1997 to $51.83 in August 1998. In other words, during the 12 months immediately preceding a 43 percent rise in the S&P 500, earnings forecasts rose just 4.8 percent! By the end of the rally in June 1999, consensus forward earnings stood at $54.75, just 5.6 percent higher than they had been in August 1998.

Consider another sharp move in the stock market, this time in the opposite direction. The middle of 2002 was one of the worst periods for stocks during the 2000–2002 bear market. From the end of May 2002 through the end of October 2002, the S&P 500 cratered 17 percent. What happened to forward earnings during the 12 months immediately preceding this collapse? Earnings forecasts fell only 1.8 percent from $56.56 in May 2001 to $55.51 in May 2002, a difference of just over one dollar! Anyone hoping for a warning of the impending plunge from earnings forecasts was sorely disappointed. During the plunge itself, earnings forecasts dropped from $55.51 in May 2002 to $54.64 in October 2002, a decline of just 1.6 percent.

Finally, consider the first year of the bull market that began in March 2003. From the end of March 2003 through the end of March 2004, the

TABLE 5.1 Consensus Forward
Earnings for S&P 500, August 1997
to June 1999

Month	Earnings
August 1997	$49.45
September 1997	$49.74
October 1997	$50.15
November 1997	$50.41
December 1997	$50.65
January 1998	$50.98
February 1998	$50.78
March 1998	$50.61
April 1998	$50.76
May 1998	$51.25
June 1998	$51.41
July 1998	$51.68
August 1998	$51.83
September 1998	$52.18
October 1998	$51.78
November 1998	$51.64
December 1998	$51.20
January 1999	$51.37
February 1999	$51.85
March 1999	$52.16
April 1999	$53.01
May 1999	$54.06
June 1999	$54.75

Source: Thomson Financial.

S&P 500 surged 33 percent. Were consensus forward earnings anticipating this gain? Most certainly not. During the 12 months preceding the new bull market, earnings forecasts rose from $54.75 to $55.13, a gain of only 0.7 percent. Investors who relied on earnings forecasts had absolutely no warning of the new bull market to come. Only once the market began rising did the herd begin raising its estimates. From March 2003 through March 2004, earnings forecasts rose 16.4 percent from $55.13 to $64.15. Unfortunately most of the upward revisions came well after most of the market's advance had already occurred.

Do you see a pattern here? Earnings forecasts completely failed to anticipate some of the most significant turns in the stock market since 1995. The value of earnings forecasts has been consistently unimpressive. Figure 5.4

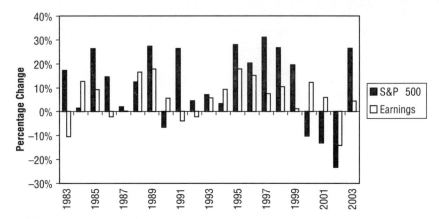

FIGURE 5.4   Percentage Change in S&P 500 versus Percentage Change in Consensus Forward Earnings for S&P 500 during Previous Year, 1983 to 2003
Source: Yahoo! Finance, Thomson Financial.

plots the annual percentage change in the S&P 500 for each year from 1983 to 2003 against the percentage change in forward earnings for the 12 months preceding each year. For example, one bar for 1983 plots the annual percentage change in the S&P 500 during 1983 (17.3 percent), while the other bar for 1983 plots the change in forward earnings from December 1981 to December 1982 (–10.4 percent).

During 13 out of the 21 years in the graph, the change in forward earnings differed from the change in the S&P 500 by more than 10 percentage points. Moreover, the graph demonstrates that forward earnings are more often a lagging than a leading indicator. For example, the S&P 500 declined 6.6 percent in 1990, while forward earnings for the previous 12 months rose 5.5 percent. What happened during the next year? While S&P 500 popped 26.3 percent, the herd was looking in the rearview mirror, and forward earnings fell 3.8 percent during 1990. The same backward-looking phenomenon occurred during the technology bubble. While the S&P 500 fell 10.1 percent in 2000, consensus forward earnings rose 12.2 percent during 1999 as the bubble continued to inflate. The herd remained optimistic during 2000, raising its earnings forecast 5.8 percent. The S&P 500, on the other hand, declined 13.0 percent in 2001. The herd turned negative only in 2001, lowering earnings forecast by 14.1 percent. By the first day of trading in 2001, however, the Nasdaq was already 55 percent below its all-time closing high. Investors who were waiting for earnings forecasts to give them advance notice of the brutal bear market were badly burned.

What about comparing changes in the S&P 500 with changes in forward earnings over the same period? Even if forward earnings cannot forecast stock prices a year in advance, surely they ought to rise and fall along with the S&P 500. Figure 5.5 shows they do not.

Not only do forward earnings fail to anticipate the movement of the stock market in advance, they do not even rise and fall in tandem with the stock market. The change in forward earnings differed from the change in the S&P 500 by more than 10 percentage points during 13 out of the 21 years in the graph—the same number of years in the previous graph. The relationship between forward earnings and the S&P 500 for any given year—whether one compares the change in the S&P 500 to the change in forward earnings during the previous year or during the current year—is nearly random.

One final example will drive home our point that earnings do not drive stock prices. In March 2000, consensus forward earnings for the S&P 500 stood at $59.30. On March 24, 2000, the S&P 500 reached an all-time closing high of 1,527.46. Move forward four years to March 2004. At this point, consensus forward earnings for the S&P 500 stood at $64.15—8.2 percent higher than they were in March 2000. Yet the S&P 500 ended March 2004 at 1,126.21—26.3 percent lower than the all-time record close in March 2000. If you use Wall Street earnings forecasts to guide your investment decisions, you might as well be playing Russian roulette.

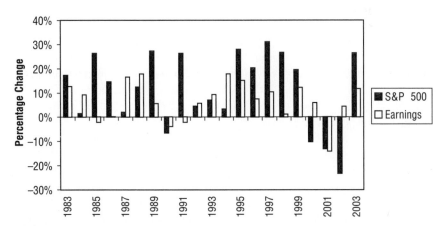

FIGURE 5.5 Percentage Change in S&P 500 versus Percentage Change in Consensus Forward Earnings for S&P 500 during Current Year, 1983 to 2003
Source: Yahoo! Finance, Thomson Financial.

GAPS IN THE CHINESE WALL

There are two other reasons why earnings estimates from securities analysts and public companies are a poor forecasting tool. One of them is that inherent conflicts of interest exist at Wall Street brokerage firms, where most analysts are employed. These firms exist to sell products—particularly new offerings and asset management services—not to produce securities research. Their research is simply a marketing tool to advance their primary mission to sell as many products as possible. As difficult as it may be to believe these days, Wall Street research used to enjoy some respect. Research departments were primarily supported by brokerage commissions, which once amounted to a hefty 25 cents per share. In May 1975, however, the New York Stock Exchange deregulated brokerage commission rates, which soon plunged 80 percent to 5 cents per share. As a result, brokerage firms could no longer use brokerage commissions to support research departments, so they turned to investment banking to generate revenue. Investment bankers, who are basically glorified salespeople, eventually gained influence over analysts, and they began to use analysts' research for sales purposes. During the stock market bubble of the late 1990s, many analysts issued favorable reviews of certain stocks—even though they realized they were poor investments—because they were rewarded or pressured by their firms to do so. Analysts such as Henry Blodget and Jack Grubman faced harsh fines and other penalties from regulators because they published overly favorable reports on companies from which their firms sought investment banking business, even when they demonstrably held contrary private opinions. After the bubble burst, Wall Street brokerages reaffirmed their commitment to a "Chinese wall" separating investment banking and research, but it does not seem to have significantly improved the quality of research. According to Zacks Investment Research, the stocks that garnered the lowest ratings from Wall Street analysts outperformed the stocks with the highest ratings every year from 2000 to 2003. Why would you take financial advice from people with such a collectively poor track record?

Buried in the fine print of many Wall Street research reports you will find a disclosure that reads something like the following: "Our firm does and seeks to do business with companies covered in its research reports. As a result, investors should be aware that the firm may have a conflict of interest that could affect the objectivity of this report." We do not mean to suggest most Wall Street analysts engage in fraud. But if you were running a business, would you publish negative reports about a current or potential client? Of course not! Is it any wonder Wall Street analysts are always so optimistic? They are generally writing about companies with which they seek to do business. Consciously or not, this conflict of interest affects their research.

COUNTING THE BEANS

The third reason why earnings are a poor forecasting tool is that public companies can often manipulate their earnings. We are not mainly concerned here with illegal activities, such as falsifying financial statements or disguising payouts to senior executives as legal or accounting fees. No amount of legislation will prevent these types of fraud because the people who perpetrate them do not care about the laws they break or the people they injure. A much broader problem than outright fraud is that companies can choose among different measures of earnings to suit their own purposes. There are four main types of earnings, each of which has its own rules for which items to include and exclude:

1. *Reported earnings.* Reported earnings are calculated according to generally accepted accounting principles. These earnings figures are used in filings with the U.S. Securities and Exchange Commission (SEC). While the use of reported earnings in SEC filings might appear to lend them credibility, they allow plenty of room for manipulation. For example, a company might classify some normal operating expenses as "unusual expenses," excluding them from expenses to lift its reported earnings. Similarly, it might not report the costs of employee stock options as an expense. Only careful scrutiny of the footnotes of SEC filings and annual reports can reveal the assumptions a company uses to calculate reported earnings.
2. *Operating earnings.* To overcome various problems with reported earnings, operating earnings were introduced. Operating earnings exclude unusual one-time events—such as merger and acquisition activity, insurance settlement payments, and sales of equipment—from net income in an attempt to determine net income from core operations. Analysts often use operating earnings to project future earnings and compare earnings between companies. Still, comparisons remain difficult because everyone has his or her own rules for what should be included and excluded from operating earnings. In addition, some companies game the system by including operating expenses as one-time charges, thus boosting their operating earnings.
3. *Pro forma earnings.* The Latin phrase *pro forma* (as a matter of form) indicates that a company made various assumptions to derive its earnings figure. Often pro forma earnings exclude the impact of mergers

and acquisitions. For example, if a company sold a division, it might exclude that division's income and expenses from its historical earnings figures to compare its current results with its historical results. Pro forma earnings are so loosely defined that they can be used to conceal almost anything from investors. Companies often use pro forma earnings to exclude some expenses management feels are nonrecurring and would provide a distorted view of the company's true earnings. Of course, if nonrecurrent expenses appear too frequently, it can be a sign that management is using pro forma earnings to smooth earnings results and appease Wall Street analysts.

4. *Core earnings.* Finally, Standard & Poor's has developed a measure called core earnings, which attempts to measure the after-tax earnings generated from the principal businesses of a corporation. Perhaps the most significant differences between core earnings and reported earnings are how these measures account for pension plans and stock options. Unlike reported earnings, which allow companies to count the long-term average gains they expect to realize on their pension plan assets as income, core earnings exclude pension plan gains from income and include pension plan costs in expenses. Unlike reported earnings, core earnings require companies to treat employee stock option grants as an expense. Finally, core earnings include restructuring charges and exclude goodwill impairment charges, gains or losses from asset sales, expenses related to mergers and acquisitions, litigation and insurance settlement costs and proceeds, and unrealized gains from hedging operations. Core earnings are basically another version of pro forma earnings as Standard & Poor's chooses to define them.

There is another metric widely used in the media, technology, and telecommunications sectors: earnings before interest, taxes, depreciation, and amortization (EBITDA) which is calculated as follows:

$$\text{EBITDA} = \text{Operating Income} + \text{Interest} + \text{Taxes} + \text{Depreciation} + \text{Amortization}$$

In other words, EBITDA measures a company's profitability before noncash charges and nonoperating expenses. It is frequently reported when companies have large amounts of fixed assets subject to depreciation or when companies have acquired intangible assets subject to amortization. EBITDA eliminates the impact of financing and capital investments on profitability, which supposedly makes comparisons across sectors easier. EBITDA first became commonplace during the leveraged buyouts of the 1980s, when it was used to gauge the ability of companies to service their debts. Now a wide range of companies report EBITDA. Some of these firms operate in sectors that require expensive assets to be depreciated or amortized over long periods, but many others—particularly technology companies—report EBITDA even though it is inappropriate to their businesses. Charlie Munger, vice chairman of Berkshire Hathaway, reportedly referred to EBITDA as "bullshit earnings" at the Berkshire Hathaway shareholders meeting in May 2003, and we could not agree more. No matter what a company's business, excluding interest, taxes, depreciation, and amortization from a company's operating income provides a highly misleading picture of a company's financial health.

We are interested in one form of earnings for the companies in which we contemplate investing: free cash flow per share. Free cash flow per share consists of after-tax earnings plus all noncash charges minus required capital expenditures, divided by the number of shares outstanding. Most stocks we buy have positive free cash flow and balance sheets on which cash and near-cash items in current assets are equal to or greater than both short-term and long-term debt. To invest in a company whose liabilities exceed its cash holdings, we must be strongly convinced that Wall Street is seriously underestimating its growth rate. For stock market liquidity purposes, free cash flow is the most important metric of a public company because it determines whether a public company will buy back shares in the open market or will need to sell shares to raise money.

Do earnings computations sound confusing? Trust us, we are only scratching the surface. The Financial Accounting Standards Board, which has been the designated organization in the private sector for setting accounting standards since 1973, has published thousands of pages of statements and interpretations clarifying various accounting techniques. Unfortunately accounting sleights-of-hand are relatively easy to implement and bury in the footnotes of SEC filings and annual reports, if they are mentioned at all. No matter what variety of earnings a company chooses to use, earnings can mean just about whatever corporate accountants and attorneys want them to mean. Investing your hard-earned assets based on earnings projections from companies and Wall Street analysts, with a few notable exceptions, is a losing game.

Detecting accounting fraud and earnings manipulations, even at large publicly traded firms, is extremely difficult. Consider one of the most infamous companies in American history: Enron. Formed in 1985, Enron's main business was buying gas and electricity from generators and selling it to consumers. In less than two decades, it became the seventh-largest public company by revenue in the United States and the largest buyer and seller of natural gas in the world. Enron attracted bright graduates of leading universities and introduced them to an aggressive, no-holds-barred corporate culture. In the mid-1990s, Enron chief executive officer Jeffrey Skilling touted Enron as an "asset-light" firm that could create profitable markets for trading nearly anything: water, advertising space, broadband capacity, even weather conditions. Enron's burgeoning trading operations were widely admired on Wall Street. In the late 1990s, Skilling and Enron chairman Kenneth Lay elicited buy ratings from nearly every Wall Street analyst who covered the company. One analyst who did not issue such a recommendation, John Olson, lost his job at Merrill Lynch in 1998 because he refused to go along with the crowd. Meanwhile, Enron enjoyed all of the outward trappings of corporate success. Houston's downtown baseball stadium was even named Enron Field in April 1999.

Behind all of the flash lurked plenty of trash, and the company finally collapsed like a house of cards. On October 16, 2001, Enron announced a third-quarter loss of $618 million and a staggering $1.2 billion loss from hundreds of complex special purpose entities created to hide Enron's debt. The SEC almost immediately launched an investigation of these partnerships, many of which had colorful names inspired by *Star Wars* characters. On November 8, 2001, Enron admitted it had overstated its profits by nearly $600 million since 1996. As a result of these revelations, Enron's smaller rival, Dynegy, withdrew from a proposed $8.4 billion merger deal. On December 2, 2001, less than two months after the announcement of its massive third quarter loss, Enron filed what at the time was the largest corporate bankruptcy petition in United States history.

The tragic results of the accounting fraud at Enron are well known. Thousands of Enron employees lost their jobs after the company's bankruptcy. Many of them also lost much of the retirement savings they had invested in Enron's 401(k) retirement plan. Sixty-two percent of this plan was invested in Enron stock, which traded well below $1 per share by the end of December 2001. Yet as Enron's stock price was tumbling, top executives were enriching themselves. During the first eight months of 2001—immediately before Enron's problems were made public—Lay and Skilling alone exercised a total of $31.7 million in stock options. In November 2001, nearly 500 Enron executives deemed critical to the company's operations received bonus payments totaling $100 million even as ordinary workers were left with little or no severance benefits.

Enron is one of the worst examples of self-dealing in the history of American business, but nearly everyone on Wall Street missed the trouble brewing at the company. Supposedly savvy people, many of whom earn hundreds of thousands of dollars per year and enjoy all of the latest technical resources, had no idea the company was a massive fraud. Some short sellers—such as Jim Chanos, president of Kynikos Associates, and other former Market TrimTabs short selling clients—found fault with Enron's

accounting, and Peter Eavis at TheStreet.com was the first to write criti-
cally about the company and its accounting. But before October 2001, no
one was able to produce a smoking gun to make everyone a believer.

In September 2001—one month before Enron reported its massive
third-quarter loss—16 out of 17 Wall Street analysts that covered Enron
rated its stock a "strong buy" or a "buy." As the *Washington Post* reported several months after Enron's collapse, Salomon Smith Barney did
not downgrade Enron from "buy" to "market perform" until October 26,
when Enron was trading around $16. Credit Suisse First Boston rated En-
ron a "strong buy" until November 29, when the stock was trading
around $0.50. Lehman Brothers never dropped its "strong buy" rating on
the company! The example of Enron raises an obvious question: If Wall
Street analysts were oblivious to Enron's problems, do you think your
chances of avoiding similar blowups are any better? One might object that
Enron is an extreme example, but that is exactly the point! Even fraud on
the scale of Enron's went undetected for years, and millions of investors—
both direct holders of Enron stock and indirect holders of Enron stock
through mutual funds—paid dearly for it.

LIQUIDITY THEORY: A BETTER WAY TO INVEST

As this chapter has shown, making investment decisions based on earnings
projections simply does not work. The prices of stocks do not move in tandem with changes in their expected future earnings. Stock prices fluctuate
primarily due to two factors:

1. The number of shares the house adds and removes from the stock market.
2. The money the players use to buy and sell shares of stock.

Wall Street conflicts of interest and earnings manipulations by public companies themselves make fundamental analysis hazardous to your wealth.
Unlike most investment research firms, TrimTabs completely ignores what
companies say and what Wall Street analysts report. Instead, we invest
based on what the house and the players are doing in the stock market
casino. These actions—not the fundamental value of companies—drive
stock prices. The next chapter explains how to analyze them.

CHAPTER 6

The House:
Secret Corporate Power

As we discuss in the preceding chapter, liquidity theory has no use for earnings statements from public companies or earnings forecasts from Wall Street strategists because stock prices are not determined by future corporate earnings except in the very long run. Liquidity theory focuses on the actions of the house—public companies and the insiders who run them—in the stock market casino. Collectively, these actions are the single best leading indicator of the direction of the stock market because they have the greatest impact on stock market liquidity.

SECRET CORPORATE POWER

The secret power public companies wield is the power to control the trading float of their own shares. Public companies do more than just buy and sell shares—they actively control the number of shares that are traded. That is what makes them the house! The executives who run public companies sell additional shares to the public when prices are high and buy other companies or their own companies' shares when prices are low. They are in the best position to know exactly when prices are high and when they are low because they do business in their industries every day. Nevertheless, most individual corporate executives are unaware of their aggregate power. When assessing the stance of the house in the stock market casino, we pay attention to what corporate executives do and ignore what they say. It is quite interesting that as L1 begins to shrink after a stock market downturn, which means public companies have become net buyers, corporate executives often continue to express concerns about the future.

Why is the power of the house in the stock market casino mostly a secret? It is a secret partly because few investors pay any attention to the actions of the house. It is also a secret because some of what the house does is either completely unknowable or knowable only on a delayed basis.

As Chapter 4 explains, we track four types of transactions to calculate the net change in the trading float of shares (L1): new cash takeovers, new stock buybacks, new offerings, and insider selling. We use these indicators in our L1 formula (L1 = New Offerings + Insider Selling − New Stock Buybacks − $\frac{2}{3}$ New Cash Takeovers − $\frac{1}{3}$ Completed Cash Takeovers) to predict the near-term direction of the stock market. In this chapter, we explain how you can analyze these transactions to beat the stock market casino. We also show where you can find publicly available information about them.

CASH TAKEOVERS

One way shares are removed from the stock market casino is through a cash takeover. A cash takeover occurs when a public company, a private company, or a private investor uses part or all cash to acquire a public company. For example, SunTrust Banks announced that it would acquire National Commerce Financial for $5.2 billion in stock and $1.8 billion in cash on May 10, 2004. If the acquirer is a public company, as in the SunTrust example, the targeted public company (National Commerce Financial) becomes a part of the acquiring company (SunTrust Banks). If the acquirer is a private company or a group of private investors, the targeted public company becomes a private company. Cash takeovers are bullish for stock market liquidity because they decrease the trading float of shares. They indicate acquirers see more value in buying other firms than in holding cash.

When an acquirer purchases a public company with stock, the stock portion has no impact on stock market liquidity. The overall trading float of shares is unaffected because one company's stock is simply exchanged for another company's stock. In the SunTrust example, only the $1.8 billion in cash that SunTrust Banks paid for National Commerce Financial would affect our liquidity analysis. The more a takeover involves stock rather than cash, the less bullish it is for stock market liquidity. Also, takeovers of private companies have no impact on stock market liquidity, although they may indicate a certain degree of economic optimism.

As Chapter 4 explains, we distinguish between new cash takeovers and completed cash takeovers in our liquidity analysis. A new cash takeover includes the cash portion of a takeover of a public company that has just been announced. A completed cash takeover includes the cash portion of a takeover of a public company that has just been completed.

When evaluating the liquidity impact of new cash takeovers, we need to consider both the dollar amount and the number. Table 6.1 shows general guidelines we use in evaluating new cash takeovers. Note that new cash takeovers are only one factor in our liquidity analysis. We do not include a similar table for completed cash takeovers. Completed cash takeovers are far less important in our liquidity analysis than new cash takeovers because they have only half of the impact in our liquidity formula of new cash takeovers, and completed cash takeovers are a backward-looking indicator.

In our liquidity analysis of new cash takeovers, we must reconcile the weekly dollar amount with the weekly number. The weekly number is generally a better indicator of corporate bullishness or corporate bearishness than the dollar amount, since one or two large new cash takeovers can easily inflate the weekly dollar amount even if little other new cash takeover activity is occurring. For example, Cingular announced on February 17, 2004, that it would acquire AT&T Wireless for $41 billion in cash. Despite the huge dollar amount of this deal, which had been planned for months and had been mostly discounted by Wall Street, it was the only substantial cash takeover announced during that month. In fact, we turned bearish at the end of February 2004 because new offerings were soaring and the usual year-end inflows of cash typically slow by March. A few large cash takeovers in a week do not signal general corporate bullishness. A week in which 10 cash takeovers totaling $5 billion are announced indicates far more corporate bullishness than a week in which one cash takeover for $6 billion is announced.

In our liquidity formula, we count two-thirds of new cash takeovers

TABLE 6.1 Guidelines for New Cash Takeovers

Weekly Dollar Amount	Stance
<$2 billion	Bearish
$2 billion to $3 billion	Somewhat bearish
$3 billion to $4 billion	Somewhat bullish
>$4 billion	Bullish

Weekly Number	Stance
<4	Bearish
4 to 5	Somewhat bearish
6 to 7	Somewhat bullish
>7	Bullish

and one-third of completed cash takeovers. Arbitrageurs generally snap up about two-thirds of the trading float of a target company almost immediately after a deal is announced. These traders hope to profit from the difference between the current stock price of the target company and the price the acquiring company has announced it will pay for each share of the target company's stock. That is why the stock of a target company often surges immediately after a deal is announced. When Cingular announced that it would pay $15 in cash for each share of AT&T Wireless, AT&T Wireless shares immediately popped nearly 20 percent to around $14 as arbitrageurs bought up much of the trading float. These arbitrageurs were taking a calculated risk that this deal would get done and that they would be able to profit from the difference between the price they paid for each AT&T Wireless share and the $15 that Cingular had promised to pay for each AT&T Wireless share. In this case, their risk was rewarded, as AT&T Wireless shareholders approved the deal on May 19, 2004. Of course, we cannot know exactly when the shares of the target company are removed from the trading float, but we believe counting two-thirds of new cash takeovers in current liquidity closely approximates what actually occurs in the stock market.

STOCK BUYBACKS

The most common way public companies buy shares in the stock market casino is through stock buybacks. A stock buyback is exactly what the words suggest—a public company buys back part of its own trading float. For example, suppose Cisco Systems has a trading float of 7 billion shares and it announces a $5 billion stock buyback over a 24-month period. This announcement means Cisco will allocate $5 billion of its own capital to repurchase its own stock over a 24-month period. The number of shares of the 7 billion share trading float Cisco repurchases depends on the price of Cisco stock at the time Cisco makes its repurchases. If the average price Cisco pays to repurchase its stock is $20 per share over the 24-month period, then Cisco will have bought back 250 million shares ($5 billion ÷ $20 per share = 250 million shares), and its trading float will be reduced to 6.75 billion shares from 7 billion shares. Assuming investors' demand for Cisco shares is unchanged, this reduction in the trading float of shares is bullish because the same amount of cash is chasing fewer shares, and future profits are spread among fewer shares.

A public company can buy back its shares on the open market or through a self-tender, also known as a dutch auction. In an open market buyback, a public company simply purchases its own shares at prevailing market prices just like any other investor. In a self-tender, a public company offers to purchase shares of its stock from current shareholders at a specified price. Sometimes a public company specifies a minimum number of outstanding shares that must be tendered for the self-tender to proceed or the maximum number of outstanding shares it will buy back.

We track only new stock buyback announcements. Actual stock buybacks can be tracked only through annual 10-K filings (audited reports of year-end financial results) and quarterly 10-Q filings (unaudited reports updating 10-K filings), which the U.S. Securities and Exchange Commission (SEC) requires all public companies to file. Aggregating this data would be extremely laborious, and the results would be months in arrears. As we discuss next, we estimate actual stock buybacks based on new stock buyback activity.

Tracking new stock buybacks is fairly straightforward. When a public company announces that it will be repurchasing a specific dollar amount of its own shares, we simply record the dollar amount of the buyback. When a public company announces that it will repurchase a specific number of shares rather than a specific dollar amount, we multiply the number of shares of the buyback by the stock price on the day before the buyback was announced. For instance, Kimberly-Clark announced an additional 25 million share repurchase program on June 8, 2004. Since Kimberly-Clark traded at about $66 on the day before this announcement was made, we record the transaction value as $1.65 billion (25 million shares × $66 per share = $1.65 billion).

When evaluating the liquidity impact of new stock buybacks, we need to consider both the dollar amount and the number. Table 6.2 shows general guidelines we use in evaluating new stock buybacks. Note that new stock buybacks are only one factor in our liquidity analysis. We must also reconcile the weekly dollar amount with the weekly number. The weekly number is generally a better indicator of corporate bullishness or bearishness than the dollar amount, since a few large-capitalization buybacks can easily inflate the weekly dollar amount even if little other activity is occurring. For example, three buybacks for $13.1 billion were announced during the five days ended Thursday, April 1, 2004. While the number was bearish, the dollar amount was bullish. We gave far more weight to the low number than the high dollar amount. If corporate America were truly bullish, we would expect far more than three buybacks to be announced in a week. By contrast, 26 buybacks for $4.5 billion were announced during the five days ended Thursday, May 20, 2004. These figures indicated far greater corporate bullishness. While the $4.5 billion dollar amount was not wildly bullish, the fact that 26 public companies saw more value in their own shares than in cash was a bullish sign.

TABLE 6.2   Guidelines for New Stock Buybacks

Weekly Dollar Amount	Stance
<$2 billion	Bearish
$2 billion to $3 billion	Somewhat bearish
$3 billion to $4 billion	Somewhat bullish
>$4 billion	Bullish

Weekly Number	Stance
<8	Bearish
8 to 14	Somewhat bearish
14 to 20	Somewhat bullish
>20	Bullish

Here is an example of how our analysis of new stock buybacks works in practice. We turned bearish at the end of February 2004 primarily because corporate buying slowed and new offerings were surging. Between March 1, 2004, and April 22, 2004, 59 buybacks for $17.7 billion were announced, a daily average of 1.3 buybacks for $400 million. Increasing stock buyback activity is typically one of the first signs the stock market may be turning upward. From April 23, 2004, through May 28, 2004, 113 buybacks for $31.2 billion were announced, a daily average of 4.3 buybacks for $1.2 billion. This development turned us bullish beginning on May 24, 2004. Remember, market turns often lag pickups in buybacks by at least several weeks.

When public companies announce a new stock buyback, they often state the period over which they will actually repurchase shares. Generally this period is between 12 and 24 months. The largest public companies have historically bought back all of the shares they announce, but smaller, less financially secure firms do not always complete their announced buybacks. Thus, we guess that at least 90 percent of announced buybacks are actually completed. While we can track new stock buyback announcements in near real time, we have no way to know when companies actually buy back their own shares except through annual 10-K filings and quarterly 10-Q filings, which are released months in arrears. In the past, we have asked the SEC to require companies to report actual stock buybacks no later than one week after they actually occur, but the SEC has yet to impose any such regulation.

To estimate actual stock buyback activity, we use the relationship between the number and dollar amount of new stock buybacks over the previous four weeks and the historic averages of the number and dollar amount of new stock buybacks. Over the two years ending May 2004, daily new stock buyback activity averaged 3.2 new stock buybacks for $700 million. We use these averages as the starting point for our estimates. If the dollar amount of new stock buybacks has been high—averaging $1 billion daily over the previous four weeks—and the number of buybacks has also been high—averaging four daily over the previous four weeks—then we would estimate actual stock buybacks are running about $900 million daily, which is somewhat higher than the daily average over the previous two years. If the dollar amount of new stock buybacks has been low—averaging $400 million daily over the previous four weeks—and the number of buybacks has also been low—averaging one daily over the previous four weeks—then we would estimate actual stock buybacks are running around $400 million daily. If the number and the dollar amount of new stock buybacks present a mixed picture—averaging two buybacks for $1.1 billion daily—then we generally give more weight to the number than to the dollar amount. In this case, we would estimate actual buybacks are running around $600 million daily. Our estimate of actual stock buybacks smoothes the fluctuations resulting from just a few large-capitalization buyback announcements over a short period of time.

NEW OFFERINGS

New offerings are by far the most important way the house sells shares in the stock market casino. We count four types in our calculation of new offerings:

1. *Initial public offerings (IPOs).* An IPO is a sale by a newly public company of shares of common stock to the public for the first time.
2. *Secondary offerings.* A secondary offering is a sale by a public company of additional shares of its common stock.
3. *Convertible bond offerings.* A convertible bond is a bond that can be exchanged at the option of the holder for a certain number of shares of a public company's common stock or preferred stock. Convertible bonds generally carry much lower interest rates than ordinary bonds because they gain value as the price of the underlying stock increases.
4. *Convertible preferred stock offerings.* Convertible preferred stock is preferred stock that can be exchanged at the option of the holder for a certain number of shares of a company's common stock. Unlike common stock, preferred stock provides a fixed dividend that is paid

to holders before any dividends are paid to holders of common stock. Also, preferred stock does not offer the voting rights of common stock.
5. *American depositary receipts (ADRs).* An ADR is a certificate issued by a U.S. bank that represents a specified number of shares of a non-U.S. stock traded on a U.S. stock exchange.

We do not count shares of non-U.S. companies sold outside the United States, since we are only concerned with the trading float of shares in the U.S. stock market. Finally, we do not count closed-end U.S. equity or bond funds as new offerings. A closed-end fund is a mutual fund that issues a fixed number of shares to the public in an IPO. Unlike an open-end fund, which is required to issue new shares and redeem outstanding shares as investors demand, shares of a closed-end fund are bought and sold on a stock exchange. We consider closed-end funds to be neutral for liquidity.

New offerings are bearish for stock market liquidity because they increase the trading float of shares. As a result, all else being equal, the same amount of cash chases more shares, and profits are spread among more shares. Institutional investors must buy nearly every IPO Wall Street underwriters offer if they want to be considered to purchase the choicest IPOs. The more shares IPOs add to the stock market, the less money institutional investors have available to buy existing shares.

Over the long term, IPOs are more bearish than secondary offerings. When a company goes public, it typically sells between 10 percent and 20 percent of its total capitalization. Insiders who own the remaining shares must wait a certain period of time—usually six months or so—for their shares to unlock before they are free to sell them. When insiders flood the stock market with unlocking shares, they can turn liquidity very bearish very fast. At the end of 1999, we estimated that the dollar value of shares that would be unlocking in 2000 from IPOs that debuted in 1999 would exceed $800 billion. Obviously nowhere near $800 billion in cash was available to buy these shares from insiders, although the public certainly tried to buy as many of them as possible through April 2000. Most of this $800 billion evaporated as the technology bubble burst.

When evaluating the liquidity impact of new offerings, we need to consider both the dollar amount and the number. Table 6.3 shows general guidelines we use in evaluating new offerings. Note that new offerings are only one factor in our liquidity analysis. While we track both the number and the dollar amount of new offerings, we give slightly more weight to the dollar amount than we do to the number of deals in our liquidity analysis. For example, a week with 25 new offerings for $3 billion is far less bearish than a week with 12 new offerings for $8 billion. The amount

TABLE 6.3   Guidelines for New Offerings

Weekly Dollar Amount	Stance
<$3 billion	Bullish
$3 billion to $4 billion	Somewhat bullish
$4 billion to $5 billion	Somewhat bearish
>$5 billion	Bearish

Weekly Number	Stance
<8	Bullish
8 to 14	Somewhat bullish
14 to 20	Somewhat bearish
>20	Bearish

of cash leaving the checking accounts of stock market intermediaries is more important than the number of companies involved in selling new offerings.

Here is an example of how our analysis of new offerings works in practice. We turned bearish at the end of February 2004 partly because new offerings were surging. Between January 30, 2004, and March 25, 2004, new offerings averaged a whopping $7.1 billion weekly ($1.4 billion daily), and they never fell below $5 billion weekly. When new offerings consistently exceed $1.25 billion daily, it is a sign the market may be topping out, which is exactly what happened. Over this period, the S&P 500 declined 2.2 percent even though investors pumped $27.9 billion into U.S. equity funds during February 2004 and March 2004. Even when corporate buying is strong and inflows are heavy, it is difficult for the stock market to head higher when new offerings exceed $1.25 billion daily.

INSIDER SELLING

Insider selling is the most difficult type of corporate liquidity transaction to track. Insider selling occurs when directors, officers, and employees exercise stock options or sell shares of their own company's stock. The SEC currently requires major insiders—officers, directors, and holders of more than 10 percent of a company's outstanding shares—to file Form 144 (Report of Proposed Sale of Securities) to report exercises of stock options no later than the date on which they intend to sell the shares. The filing of Form 144 does not necessarily mean the sale was actually completed, and

Form 144 is not required to be filed when the amount of stock intended for sale during any three-month period does not exceed 500 shares and the aggregate sale value does not exceed $10,000. Major insiders also must file Form 4 (Statement of Changes in Beneficial Ownership of Securities) with the SEC when they buy or sell stock or exercise stock options. The deadline for filing Form 4 is the tenth day of the month following the transaction. All transactions under $10,000 during a month and all gifts of stock are exempt from this reporting requirement. Significantly, insiders below the level of corporate vice president are not required to report any transactions to the SEC. In the past, we have asked the SEC to require companies to report the dollar amount of all insider sales, but the SEC has yet to impose any such regulation.

This regulatory framework presents two major problems for investors who wish to track insider selling. First, smaller transactions by major insiders and all transactions by insiders below the level of corporate vice president are completely exempt from reporting. Second, it is extremely time-consuming to aggregate this data. We explain next how we manage these difficulties.

Table 6.4 shows general guidelines we use in evaluating insider selling. Note that insider selling is only one factor in our liquidity analysis. At TrimTabs, we estimate insider selling by doubling the dollar amount of Form 144 shares sold as reported by Thomson Financial. Since insiders below the level of corporate vice president are not required to report transactions to the SEC, we estimate that selling by these insiders is at least equal to the dollar amount of Form 144 shares sold. If anything, our method of doubling of Form 144 insider selling underestimates insider selling.

Insider selling generally falls within a relatively narrow range. While some insider selling occurs because of stock market fluctuations, a certain level of natural selling occurs throughout the year.

TABLE 6.4   Guidelines for Insider Selling

Weekly Dollar Amount	Stance
<$2.5 billion	Bullish
$2.5 billion to $3.0 billion	Somewhat bullish
$3.0 billion to $3.5 billion	Somewhat bearish
>$3.5 billion	Bearish

SHORT-TERM LIQUIDITY FORECASTS

Estimating the daily cash flow into and out of the stock market for the upcoming week is a powerful forecasting tool. We use a modified version of our liquidity formula to estimate daily cash flow:

Estimated Daily L1 = New Offerings + Insider Selling
$\qquad$ – Actual Stock Buybacks – $^2/_3$ New Cash Takeovers

Here is how we compute the four components of this formula:

1. *New offerings.* We estimate daily new offerings according to the dollar amount of new offerings scheduled on the calendar at the beginning of the week. We obtain this information each week from Dealogic, a capital markets research firm. To account for secondary offerings that are not scheduled at the beginning of the week, many of which are priced the night before or even the morning of their sale, we generally double the dollar amount of new offerings scheduled. For example, if Dealogic reports $2.5 billion in new offerings on the new offering calendar for the upcoming week, we would estimate new offerings at $1 billion daily ($2.5 billion × 2 ÷ 5 days = $1 billion).
2. *Insider selling.* We estimate daily insider selling based on our estimate of the level of insider selling over the previous eight weeks. For example, if we estimated that insider selling averaged $3 billion weekly over the previous eight weeks, we would estimate insider selling at $600 million daily ($3 billion ÷ 5 days = $600 million).
3. *Actual stock buybacks.* We estimate daily actual stock buybacks by modifying the daily average of new stock buybacks over the previous two years according to the level of new stock buyback activity over the previous four weeks. For example, if the daily average of new stock buybacks were $800 million daily over the previous two years and both the number and dollar amount of new stock buybacks over the previous four weeks were extremely light, we would estimate actual stock buybacks at $400 million daily.
4. *New cash takeovers.* We estimate daily new cash takeovers based on the average of daily new cash takeovers over the previous four weeks. We multiply this figure by 67 percent because we count two-thirds of the dollar amount of new cash takeovers in current liquidity. For example, if new cash takeovers averaged $700 million daily over the previous four weeks, we would estimate new cash takeovers at $500 million daily ($700 million × .67 = $500 million).

Here is an example from the May 24, 2004, issue of *TrimTabs Weekly Liquidity* of how we forecast stock market liquidity on a short-term basis:

> *Tracking daily cash flow into and out of the stock market shows that corporate liquidity has improved dramatically. New cash takeovers have added an average of $700 million daily to current liquidity over the past four weeks. Due to the pickup in stock buyback announcements over the past four weeks, we estimate that actual stock buybacks are running at a $900 million daily pace, which is higher than the $650 million daily average of new stock buybacks over the past two years. Adding $700 million daily from new cash takeovers to $900 million daily in actual buybacks, we estimate that corporate buying totals $1.6 billion daily.*
>
> *On the other side of the corporate liquidity ledger, we expect at least $1.4 million daily in new offerings and $400 million daily of insider selling during this coming week. Thus, corporate selling should total $1.8 billion daily, which leaves a $200 million daily liquidity gap.*

Expressed in our modified liquidity formula, our daily cash flow estimate for the week of May 24, 2004, would be:

Estimated Daily L1 = $1.4 Billion + $400 Million – $900 Million
– $700 Million = $200 Million

Based on this formula, we would likely be cautiously bearish for the week ahead. If we expected strong U.S. equity fund inflows or a major new cash takeover was announced over the previous weekend, then we might turn neutral. If we expected heavy U.S. equity fund outflows, then we might turn fully bearish. After all, liquidity analysis remains an art as well as a science.

WHERE TO FIND THE DATA

Much of the data mentioned in this chapter is available to the public. TrimTabs tracks new cash takeovers and new stock buybacks using data provided by Dealogic (data available only to subscribers) and The Online Investor (www.theonlineinvestor.com). Bloomberg News (www.bloomberg.com), CBS MarketWatch (www.cbsmarketwatch.com), Thomson Financial (data available only to subscribers), and Yahoo! Finance (http://finance.yahoo.com) also provide information on cash takeovers and stock buybacks. TrimTabs reports the number and dollar amount of new cash takeovers, the dollar amount of completed cash takeovers, and the number and dollar amount of new stock buybacks in *TrimTabs Weekly Liquidity*, which is designed for professional investors, and *TrimTabs Monthly Liquidity*, which is designed for individual investors. *TrimTabs Weekly Liquidity* is available to the public on the TrimTabs web site on a delayed basis (visit www.trimtabs.com and select "Liquidity" on the sidebar).

TrimTabs tracks new offerings using data provided by Dealogic (data available only to subscribers). Some of the same information is publicly accessible in near real time at CBS MarketWatch (www.cbsmarket watch.com), CNNmoney (http://money.cnn.com), and Yahoo! Finance (http://finance.yahoo.com). *TrimTabs Weekly Liquidity* reports the number and dollar amount of new offerings each week.

TrimTabs estimates insider selling using Form 144 filings data compiled by Thomson Financial (data available only to subscribers). *TrimTabs Weekly Liquidity* and *TrimTabs Monthly Liquidity* report our estimates of insider selling for previous weeks, although only our estimate of insider selling over the previous eight weeks is available to the public on the TrimTabs web site on a delayed basis. A limited amount of aggregated insider selling data is publicly available elsewhere. Using weekly data provided by Thomson Financial, the *Wall Street Journal* reports insider buying and selling by market sector in its "Insider Trading Spotlight." Also, Thomson Financial's monthly summary of insider activity is widely reported in the financial media. To find these reports, type "Thomson insider selling" into the Google News search engine (visit www.google.com and select "News"). This monthly summary includes the dollar sell-buy ratio, which reports how many dollars of stock insiders are selling for every dollar of stock insiders are buying each month.

CHAPTER 7

The Players:
Buying, Selling, and Borrowing

While the previous chapter focuses on the actions of the house in the stock market casino, this chapter focuses on the actions of the players. To beat the stock market casino, we need to know more than what the house is doing—we also need to know what the players are doing. In 2003, L1 ballooned by $80 billion, and the house was a net seller for 8 out of 12 months. Yet the S&P 500 rose 26 percent, and the Nasdaq surged 50 percent. Why did the stock market surge even though the house was an aggressive net seller? The players were dumping money into the stock market casino at an extraordinary rate. U.S. equity fund inflows totaled $129 billion, or $10.7 billion per month, and at least another $129 billion probably flowed directly into equities. In addition, we estimate that pension funds and hedge funds poured at least $300 billion into the stock market beginning in the second quarter of 2003. In sum, well over half a trillion dollars flowed into equities in 2003, which was more than sufficient to offset net corporate selling. The extraordinary returns of 2003, which came despite steady corporate selling, are a good example of why liquidity theory examines the actions of the players as well as the house. While the actions of the house are the best leading indicator of the stock market's direction, the actions of the players can overwhelm them if they reach extreme levels. This chapter explains how to analyze the actions of the players and where you can find publicly available information about them.

MUTUAL FUNDS FLOWS

We track what the players are doing in the stock market casino by monitoring flows into and out of equity mutual funds. We readily acknowledge that equity mutual funds flows are an imperfect measure of the cash the players are investing or withdrawing from stocks, since the players can also invest in stocks by buying stocks directly or by buying exchange-traded funds (ETFs). Nevertheless, as we have tracked liquidity over the years, we have found that mutual funds flows are a reasonably good proxy for the actions of the players in the stock market casino.

Unlike the net change in the trading float of shares (L1), U.S. equity fund flows (L2) are a contrary indicator. In other words, it is a bearish sign when U.S. equity funds post heavy inflows and a bullish sign when U.S. equity funds post heavy outflows. L2 is a particularly useful indicator when it reaches extreme levels over an extended period. Low flows and flows over short periods are not particularly meaningful.

Investing the way most individual investors invest is much like driving a car with your hands on the steering wheel, your foot on the gas pedal, and your eyes on the rearview mirror. Individual investors tend to assume that trends in the recent past will continue into the future. By the time they pile into the latest hot stock or sector, most of the gains have already occurred. When U.S. equity funds post heavy inflows, many investors have already turned bullish. Since many investors have already put money to work, less cash will likely be available in the future to take the market higher. The converse is equally true. When U.S. equity funds post heavy outflows, many investors have already turned bearish. Since many investors have already sold heavily, less cash will likely be pulled from the market in the future. You cannot invest successfully by matching mutual funds flows because the players are the dumb money in the stock market casino. When the actions of the players reach extreme levels, you need to do the opposite of what they are doing to make money.

Where to Find the Data

The authoritative source of mutual funds flow data is the Investment Company Institute (ICI), the mutual fund trade group. The ICI releases funds flow data on its web site at www.ici.org/stats/mf/index.html#TopOfPage. The release, entitled "Trends in Mutual Fund Investing," provides flow data for stock, bond, and money market funds. The data is compiled monthly and released on a delay of about one month (e.g., January's data is released in late February).

The ICI release contains a wealth of information based on data from 8,300 U.S.-based equity mutual funds. For liquidity purposes, the net flows of stock and bond funds are most significant. This information appears in the "Highlights" section immediately after the "Net Assets of Mutual Funds" table. For example, in January 2004, the ICI reported that stock funds posted an inflow of $43.76 billion and bond funds posted an inflow of $496 million. The ICI's results are also widely reported in the financial media, including the *Wall Street Journal* and *Investor's Business Daily*.

Of course, this ICI data has two major shortcomings. First, it is only released on a monthly basis on a delay of about one month. Second, it does not break down funds flow data into categories. Both TrimTabs and AMG Data Services make a limited amount of free weekly funds flow data available to the public. Each issue of *Barron's* reports AMG Data Services' estimates of the four-week moving averages of net cash flow into stock, bond, and money market funds. In addition, TrimTabs and AMG Data Services issue press releases on weekly funds flow that are regularly reported in the financial media, including TheStreet.com (www.thestreet.com) and CBS MarketWatch (www.cbsmarketwatch.com). Investors who do not subscribe to a funds flow tracking service can easily access data on funds flow on a weekly and monthly basis.

How to Interpret the Data

TrimTabs provides a wealth of detailed daily funds flow data to its subscribers, and this discussion of funds flow is based on this data. There is currently no way to track flows at every one of the thousands of funds available, which include about 4,700 equity funds alone. So we track flows at about 80 fund families on a daily basis. These fund families have assets equal to 15 percent of all ICI equity fund assets and 13 percent of all ICI bond fund assets. We regress these numbers by sector to estimate daily flows for various categories according to capitalization, objective, and sector. Each day, we report this information to our subscribers in *TrimTabs Daily Mutual Funds Flow*. Two weeks after the end of each month, we revise our monthly flow estimates using data provided by Charles Schwab as well as Fidelity, Janus, MFSS, and Vanguard, the largest four fund families whose funds are not among the U.S. equity funds we track daily.

Funds flow is a lagging contrary indicator that is most useful in liquidity analysis when it reaches extreme levels. Flows for U.S. equity funds are most important in our liquidity analysis. When flows reach extreme levels in either direction, a market turning point is likely not far off. Two recent examples illustrate this point.

From October 1999 to March 2000, investors poured $152 billion, or $21.7 billion per month, into U.S. equity funds. Figure 7.1 plots monthly U.S. equity fund flows against the S&P 500 from October 1999 to December 2000. Not surprisingly, the technology bubble peaked in March 2000. When investors are piling into equities at a rate of at least $20 billion per month, it is fairly reliable sign that a market top is forming.

By contrast, consider monthly U.S. equity fund flows during 2002,

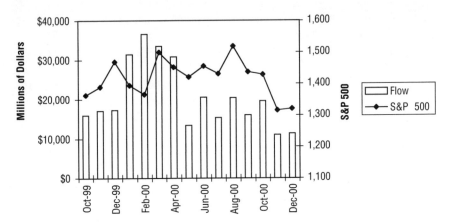

FIGURE 7.1 Monthly U.S. Equity Fund Flows versus S&P 500, October 1999 to December 2000
Source: Investment Company Institute, Yahoo! Finance.

which are plotted against the S&P 500 in Figure 7.2. The S&P 500 reached two major bottoms during this period, one in July and one October. Notice that both of these bottoms were marked by heavy U.S. equity fund outflows. When investors dump U.S. equity funds at a rate above $15 billion per month, a market bottom usually follows.

U.S. equity fund flows are a contrary indicator at extremes. Weekly flows of no more than $3 billion do not have strong predictive value. And even if flows reach this level, they cannot be analyzed in isolation. If corporate buying is strong, it can offset weak inflows, and vice versa. For example, U.S. equity funds posted an outflow of $27 billion in September 2001 and an inflow of just $5 billion in October 2001 in the wake of the September 11 attacks. Yet the market rebounded sharply from its lows because corporate America was a heavy net buyer in September 2001. During that month, L1 plunged a wildly bullish $46 billion. The cash corporate America was pumping into the market through stock buybacks was more than enough to offset weak U.S. equity fund inflows.

While U.S. equity funds are the most important funds flow indicator, we also track the percentage of all equity fund inflows heading into global equity funds to assess the prospects for international investments and the U.S. dollar. Remember, individual investors invariably buy high and sell low. When U.S. investors direct sizable proportions of their equity fund investments into global equity funds, it often means international markets are relatively expensive and the value of the U.S. dollar could be bottoming. Conversely, when U.S. investors direct nearly all of their equity fund

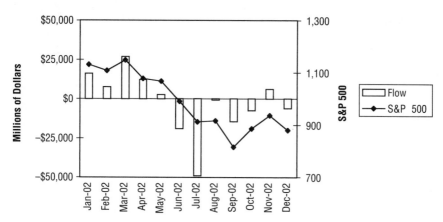

FIGURE 7.2 Monthly U.S. Equity Fund Flows versus S&P 500, January 2002 to December 2002
Source: Investment Company Institute, Yahoo! Finance.

investments into U.S. equities, it often means international markets are relatively cheap and the value of the U.S. dollar could be peaking. The percentage of all equity funds heading abroad has the most predictive value when it reaches extreme levels, which we define as less than 10 percent and greater than 30 percent. The best recent example of heavy inflows into global equity funds came in early 2004. Figure 7.3 plots global equity fund inflows as a percentage of all equity fund inflows from April 2003 to April 2004.

As the percentage of equity fund inflows heading abroad rose above 30 percent at the end of 2003, the euro hit a record high (up until then) of $1.30 against the U.S. dollar in February 2004. The percentage of all equity fund inflows heading abroad surged above 35 percent in March 2004. By the end of April 2004, however, the euro dropped to $1.18. Just as they do with U.S. equity funds, individual investors buy global equity funds high and sell them low.

Finally, we pay careful attention to unusually strong inflows and outflows in sector funds. The behavior of mutual fund investors is a remarkably good contrary indicator because they invariably chase performance. When a sector experiences extremely heavy inflows or outflows over a short period of time, it is often a signal that the sector may be topping or bottoming. The best recent example of heavy sector fund flows came in early 2004 in real estate funds. Beginning in January 2004, we measured extremely heavy inflows into the real estate funds we track daily. In fact, some of the weekly inflows exceeded a whopping 3 percent of these funds'

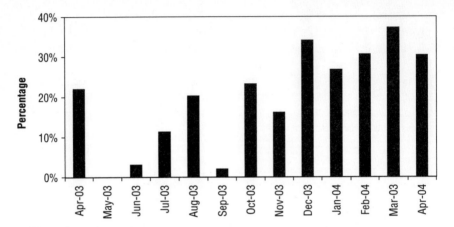

FIGURE 7.3   Global Equity Fund Inflows as a Percentage of All Equity Fund
Inflows, April 2003 to April 2004
Source: Investment Company Institute.

net assets as speculators flooded into the sector. Figure 7.4 plots weekly
real estate fund flows against the Morgan Stanley REIT Index from January 2004 to April 2004.

Note that the REIT index rose steadily during the first three months of
the year, backed by surging inflows. Appropriately enough, it peaked on
April Fool's Day, having risen 13 percent in just three months. On April 2,
the U.S. Bureau of Labor Statistics reported that 308,000 jobs were created

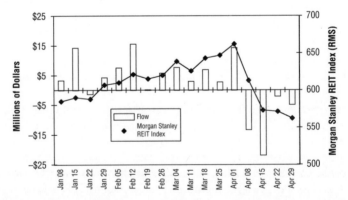

FIGURE 7.4   Weekly Real Estate Fund Flows versus Morgan Stanley REIT Index,
January 2004 to April 2004
Source: TrimTabs Investment Research, Yahoo! Finance.

in March, and the prospect of imminent Federal Reserve interest rate hikes prompted the hot money to flee the sector. Predictably, investors who had purchased real estate fund shares eagerly when the REIT index was near its peak had little interest in buying when real estate funds swooned, and inflows quickly turned to outflows by mid-April. By the end of April, the REIT index had plunged 15 percent from its April Fool's Day peak. Investors who were aware of all of the hot money flooding into real estate funds would have been spared the carnage.

FOREIGN PURCHASES AND SALES OF U.S. SECURITIES

Like mutual funds flows, foreign purchases and sales of U.S. securities are a contrary indicator that is most useful when it reaches an extreme level for an extended period. Foreign investors are no different from U.S. individual investors—they buy high and sell low.

Where to Find the Data

The U.S. Department of the Treasury releases data on foreign purchases and sales of U.S. securities on its web site. The table, entitled "Foreign Purchases and Sales of Long-Term Domestic and Foreign Securities by Type," is available at www.treas.gov/tic/s1_99996.txt. The data is compiled monthly and released on a delay of about two months (e.g., January's data is released in late March).

How to Interpret the Data

The data on foreign purchases and sales is not arranged in a particularly convenient way. The first six data columns show monthly purchases by foreigners of six assets: U.S. Treasury bonds and notes, U.S. government agency bonds, U.S. corporate bonds, U.S. corporate stocks, foreign stocks, and foreign bonds. The next six data columns show monthly sales by foreigners of these assets. All figures are shown in millions of dollars. For liquidity purposes, we are most interested in the data on U.S. stocks. To determine whether foreigners were net buyers or net sellers of U.S. stocks during a particular month, we subtract foreign sales of U.S. stocks from foreign purchases of U.S. stocks during that month. For example, in January 2004, foreigners bought $323,391,000 of U.S. stocks and sold $310,604,000 in U.S. stocks. Thus, net foreign buying of U.S. stocks was $12,787,000. We should note that flows from U.S. hedge funds domiciled offshore are included in foreign purchases and sales. Unfortunately there is no way to know what percentages of foreign purchases and sales are from offshore U.S. hedge funds.

Foreigners are even more notorious than U.S. investors for entering the U.S. stock market near peaks and abandoning it near bottoms, so this indicator is most useful when it reaches extreme levels over a period of several months. In 2000, just as the bubble was bursting, foreigners poured an all-time record $174 billion into U.S. stocks. Figure 7.5 plots foreign purchases of U.S. stocks against the S&P 500 from January 1999 to December 2000.

Note that just as the bubble peaked, foreigners were buying U.S. stocks most heavily. Foreign buying reached an all-time monthly high of $28 billion in February 2000, and the $24 billion monthly inflow in March 2000 was nearly as high. Even after the major averages had retreated from their peaks, foreigners continued to buy. From April 2000 until December 2000, foreigners pumped $113 billion, or $9.4 billion per month, into U.S. stocks, and the $24 billion inflow from foreigners in January 2001 nearly equaled the inflow in March 2000! In fact, foreigners were not net sellers of U.S. stocks until September 2001. Investors' knack for ensuring they are fully invested right before the market cracks open to the downside knows no national boundaries!

By contrast, in 2002 and 2003, foreigners bought just $49 billion and $45 billion in U.S. stocks, respectively. In other words, foreigners bought more U.S. stocks during February 2000 and March 2000 than they did during all of 2002 or 2003. In fact, foreigners were net sellers in 7 of the 24 months in 2002 and 2003. Figure 7.6 plots foreign purchases of U.S. stocks against the S&P 500 from January 2002 to December 2003.

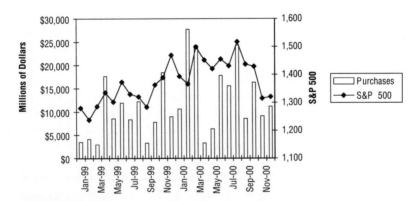

FIGURE 7.5 Net Foreign Purchases of U.S. Stocks versus S&P 500, January 1999 to December 2000
Raw data obtained from U.S. Department of the Treasury, Yahoo! Finance.

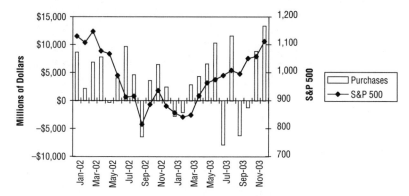

FIGURE 7.6　Net Foreign Purchases of U.S. Stocks, January 2002 to December 2003
Source: U.S. Department of the Treasury; Yahoo! Finance.

Foreign flows are most useful when they reach extreme levels. On the one hand, when foreign flows exceed $8 billion monthly for several months, a near-term top could be forming. On the other hand, when foreign flows are negative for several months, a near-term bottom could be forming.

MARGIN DEBT (L3)

Margin debt is money investors borrow at a fixed interest rate to invest. For example, an ultrahigh-net-worth individual might borrow $1 million from J. P. Morgan Private Bank at 5 percent interest to invest in oil and gas stocks. Once the investor sold these stocks, she would repay the $1 million she borrowed from J. P. Morgan Private Bank with interest, obviously hoping the return on these stocks was greater than the interest cost of the borrowed money. Margin debt is a lagging contrary indicator. Extremely rapid growth in margin debt indicates investors are becoming wildly bullish and a sell-off is likely. Conversely, extremely rapid declines in margin debt indicate investors are becoming despondent and a rally could break out soon. Like funds flows, when the herd leans strongly in one direction, a reversal usually follows.

Where to Find the Data

The New York Stock Exchange (NYSE) releases data on margin debt levels at its member firms on its web site. The table, entitled "New York Stock

Exchange Member Firms Customers' Margin Debt," is available at
www.nyse.com/pdfs/marginMMYY.pdf, in which "MM" is the two-digit
month and "YY" is the two-digit year of the most recent month the data
covers. For example, the data through August 2004 can be found at
www.nyse.com/pdfs/margin0804.pdf. The data is compiled monthly and
released on a delay of about one month (e.g., data for January is released
in late February).

How to Interpret the Data

The table is arranged in three data columns, which show monthly balances
in three categories: debit balances in margin accounts, free credit balances
in cash accounts, and free credit balances in margin accounts. All figures
are shown in millions of dollars.

For liquidity purposes, we are concerned with monthly changes in
debit balances in margin accounts. To compute monthly changes, we subtract the balance in one month from the balance in the preceding month.
For example, debit balances in January 2004 were $178,820,000, and
debit balances in February 2004 were $180,360,000. Thus, margin debt
rose in February 2004 by $1,540,000, which is only a small increase.

Margin debt is the least significant of the three liquidity trim tabs. Like
foreign purchases, it is a lagging contrary indicator that carries the most
predictive value when it reaches extreme levels. From 1995 to 1998, margin debt grew at a fairly steady pace, rising less than $30 billion per year.
As the technology bubble expanded in 1999, however, margin debt surged
by an all-time record $88 billion. Figure 7.7 plots the net change in margin
debt against the S&P 500 from January 1999 to December 2001.

From November 1999 to March 2000, margin debt ballooned by an
astonishing $96 billion, or $19.3 billion per month, an unprecedented
surge. Both the S&P 500 and the Nasdaq reached all-time closing highs in
March 2000, when margin debt peaked. Margin debt did not begin to decline significantly from its peak levels until October 2000. Even after the
major averages had peaked, the players were still borrowing to buy at
high levels.

Steep declines in margin debt are generally a bullish contrary indicator
that the market is bottoming. For example, in September 2001, margin
debt plunged $16 billion, or 10 percent, the second-highest monthly de-
cline ever recorded. Not surprisingly, the major averages rebounded
sharply from their September 21 closing lows during the next two months.
Another example of margin debt as a bullish contrary indicator came in
mid-2002. Between May 2002 and September 2002, margin debt declined
for five straight months. The total decline reached $21 billion, or $4.1 bil-

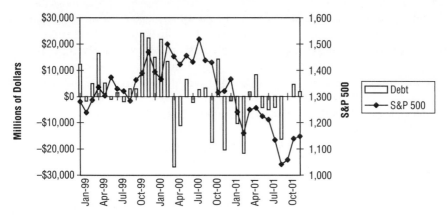

FIGURE 7.7 Net Change in Margin Debt versus S&P 500, January 1999 to December 2001
Raw data obtained from New York Stock Exchange, Yahoo! Finance.

lion per month. Figure 7.8 plots the net change in margin debt against the S&P 500 from January 2002 to December 2002. As the graph shows, the S&P 500 was hitting bear market lows during this period.

Margin debt is most useful as a liquidity indicator when it reaches extreme levels. If margin debt changes by less than $4 billion per month in either direction, its predictive value is not strong. On the one hand, if margin

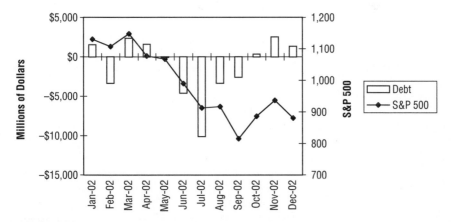

FIGURE 7.8 Net Change in Margin Debt versus S&P 500, January 2002 to December 2002
Raw data obtained from New York Stock Exchange, Yahoo! Finance.

debt grows more than $5 billion per month over several months, it indi-
cates the players are becoming increasingly bullish and the market could be
topping. On the other hand, if margin debt contracts by more than $5 bil-
lion per month over several months, it indicates the players are restraining
their speculative urges and the market could be bottoming. Obviously it
would helpful for followers of liquidity theory to have weekly or daily data
on margin debt balances. We have approached several brokerage firms for
such information, but so far we have not been able to obtain usable data.
For now, we must settle for the NYSE's monthly results.

This chapter concludes our explanation of our liquidity indicators.
Now it is time to show how liquidity played out in the stock market casino
during the recent past.

Looking Back

The Bull Market and the Bubble

Our account of stock market history begins in 1995, when TrimTabs Investment Research—or Market TrimTabs as it was known at the time—began to track stock market liquidity. On the one hand, we wish we had complete liquidity data available for years before 1995 to share with our clients and our readers. On the other hand, the period from 1995 to 2004 encompassed an astonishing range of market conditions: a raging bull market, a brutal bear market, and a fledgling recovery. Close examination of this period is a good way to learn how liquidity actually plays out in the stock market casino.

THE BULL MARKET OF THE LATE 1990s

As 1995 began, the United States was emerging from a painful recession. Few people imagined the S&P 500 and the Nasdaq would nearly triple between 1995 and 1998, but that is exactly what happened. (See Figure 8.1.) From the end of 1994 to the end of 1998, the S&P 500 rose from 459.27 to 1,229.23, a gain of 168 percent. Over the same period, the Nasdaq rose from 751.96 to 2,192.69, a gain of 192 percent. Not only were stock market gains heavy, they were remarkably consistent. The S&P 500 rose more than 20 percent for five straight years from 1995 to 1999. This type of market action is unusual. In fact, it is unlikely to occur again for another generation.

Many investment professionals and academics were at a loss to explain the dramatic escalation of stock prices during these years. By the beginning of 1999, stocks had become more expensive than at any other period in U.S. history. The dividend yield on the S&P 500 was a paltry 1.3 percent, and the trailing price-earnings (P/E) ratio of the S&P 500 was a whopping 33. Remember, stock prices reached these valuations more than a year before the technology bubble peaked! What drove the heady gains of the late

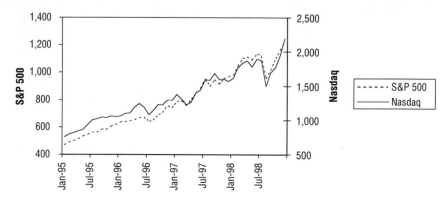

FIGURE 8.1 S&P 500 and Nasdaq, January 1995 to December 1998
Raw data obtained from Yahoo! Finance.

1990s? Stocks selling at fire sale prices? Federal Reserve chairman Alan Greenspan's deft management of the economy? President Bill Clinton's enlightened economic policies? Rampant speculation by individual investors?

None of these factors adequately explains the market's advance. According to various fundamental measures, the stock market was reasonably valued in 1995, but valuations were nowhere near as low as they were at other recent market bottoms in 1974 or 1982. Chairman Greenspan indeed presided over the Federal Reserve Board during this period, but there was nothing particularly radical about his approach during these years, and the federal funds rate oscillated in a narrow range between 4.5 percent to 6.0 percent. While President Clinton never misses an opportunity to take credit for the 1990s boom, the policies of presidents have a limited impact on the economy despite the claims of politicians to the contrary. Finally, as we discuss later, margin debt levels demonstrate that investors were not engaging in unusually wild speculation during this period. So what accounted for the stock market's meteoric rise? The answer is simple. The house in the stock market casino (public companies and the insiders who run them) was a net buyer of shares while the players (individual investors) were buying heavily, too.

The net change in the trading float of shares (L1), the best leading indicator of the direction of the stock market, was bullish every year from 1995 to 1998. L1 declined by $319 billion during these four years, an average of $80 billion per year. Public companies were using the substantial free cash flow they were generating to buy other companies and buy back their own shares. New cash takeovers increased in all but one year, rising from $89 billion in 1995 to $157 billion in 1998, and they averaged $105 billion per year. At the same time, stock buybacks were announced at a healthy, consistent pace. They totaled $522 billion, an average of $131 billion per year. Figure 8.2 shows the increasing pace of new cash takeovers and the steady pace of new stock buybacks, which were the main foundations of the bull market.

Meanwhile, the house was selling nowhere near as heavily as it was buying. New offerings rose each year from $87 billion in 1995 to $133 billion in 1997, but then they fell back to $90 billion in 1998. All told, the house sold $408 billion, an average of $102 billion per year, in fresh paper. Significantly, the house was buying back more shares than it was selling through new offerings every year from 1995 to 1998, a phenomenon that did not recur until 2004. Insider selling increased each year from 1995 to 1998 and more than doubled from $32 billion in 1995 to $69 billion in 1998. Yet even the $69 billion in insider selling in 1998 was low compared to the level of corporate buying.

Not only was the house a net buyer of $319 billion from 1995 to 1998, but the players were buying heavily, too. This combination is what produced the explosive stock market returns of the late 1990s. From 1995 to 1998, U.S. equity fund inflows (L2) totaled $621 billion. At least as much cash probably flowed into U.S. stocks directly. All told, the players dumped at least $1.2 trillion into U.S. stocks during these four years. Even as U.S. equity fund assets ballooned, U.S. equity mutual fund managers were shifting more of these assets from cash to equities. In 1995, cash levels in U.S. equity funds stood at 7.7 percent. This percentage fell every year from 1995 to 1998, declining to 4.7 percent in 1998. For comparison, cash levels at

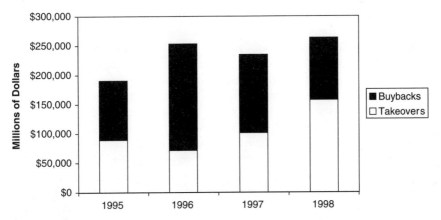

FIGURE 8.2 New Cash Takeovers and New Stock Buybacks, 1995 to 1998
Source: TrimTabs Investment Research.

U.S. equity funds stood at 3.8 percent at the height of the bubble in March 2000 and 4.1 percent in September 2004. Not only were U.S. equity funds swelling with new assets, but an increasing proportion of these assets was deployed in the stock market.

Now do you see why the late 1990s produced one of the most powerful bull markets ever? As we learned in Chapter 3, when the supply of shares steadily declines while the demand for shares surges, stock prices rise. Alan Greenspan famously warned about "irrational exuberance" in December 1996, yet liquidity theory suggests the exuberance throughout most of the late 1990s was entirely rational. The stock market advance from 1995 to 1998 was built on solid liquidity foundations, and market speculation was nowhere near the levels of 1999 and 2000. Margin debt at New York Stock Exchange (NYSE) member firms edged up slowly, and it never rose more than $30 billion during any year from 1995 to 1998. As we discuss later, "irrational exuberance" reared its head in 1999, when margin debt at NYSE member firms ballooned by a whopping $88 billion—more than it had risen during the four years from 1995 to 1998 combined! Not surprisingly, the house became a net seller by the end of 1999, just as the technology bubble was reaching fever pitch.

Why did the technology bubble grow so quickly beginning in early 1999? Why was the ride down almost as rapid? Liquidity theory holds the key to answering these questions. To better understand the bubble and the bust, we divide the heady days of the bubble into three periods: January 1999 to September 1999, October 1999 to April 2000, and May 2000 to December 2000. In each period, we show exactly how the actions of the house and the players helped inflate the bubble and then burst it.

THE RIDE UP: JANUARY 1999 TO SEPTEMBER 1999

The excesses of the technology boom were readily apparent by early 1999. Companies went public with hardly any revenues, let alone earnings, making their founders wealthy beyond their wildest dreams. Firms lured restless talent from competitors with generous grants of stock options. In fact, some employees of Internet start-ups were compensated solely with stock options. It was also a heady time on Wall Street. Investment bankers could barely keep up with the relentless demand of companies to go public. Ameritrade, E*Trade, and other online brokers became wildly popular by offering ordinary Americans an inexpensive way to take their seats in the stock market casino. Market strategists such as Abby Joseph Cohen and Ed Kerschner, who had forecast the stock market's meteoric rise in the late

1990s, were widely hailed as prophets. Few people imagined the party would come crashing to an end in little more than a year.

Yet this book is not an account of the foibles of the dot-com era. For those who are interested in this era, one of the best accounts can be found in Maggie Mahar's *Bull! A History of the Boom, 1982–1999* (HarperBusiness, 2003). Our focus in this book is on liquidity theory and how investors who used it could have profited not only during the technology bubble but also during the collapse that followed. Given the frenzied atmosphere on Wall Street in 1999, you may be surprised to learn that L1 posted a bullish $69 billion decline in that year. The stock market did not surge merely because the players were buying heavily. The house was a net buyer for most of the year. From January to September, the house announced $198 billion in cash takeovers, an average of $22 billion per month. This total was the highest amount we have ever recorded during the first nine months of the year. At the same time, the house bought back shares worth $128 billion, an average of $14 billion per month.

While the house was buying heavily, it was selling heavily, too. From January to September, the house sold $115 billion in fresh paper, an average of $13 billion per month, which was a record pace for the first nine months of the year. Investors bid up many of these new shares to lofty prices that had absolutely no regard for value, and insiders took full advantage of rising stock prices to bail out of their own companies' shares at an increasing rate. Nevertheless, the $22 billion per month in new cash takeovers and $14 billion per month in new stock buybacks were more than sufficient to offset new offerings and insider selling, even without considering inflows from the players.

Yet the house's net buying was not the primary trigger for the market's ascent. The divergence in the performance of the S&P 500 and the Nasdaq suggested something else was at work. From January to September, the S&P 500 rose from 1,229.23 to 1,282.71, a gain of just over 4 percent. Over the same period, the Nasdaq surged from 2,192.69 to 2,746.16, a gain of 25 percent. (See Figure 8.3.)

What accounted for the divergence in these indexes? The answer is simple. Investors were pouring money into the most speculative areas of the market, including the technology stocks and Internet stocks that dominated the Nasdaq. Between January and September, U.S. equity funds received $126 billion in fresh cash, an average of $14 billion per month. Direct investments into U.S. equities were probably equal to U.S. equity fund inflows, which meant over $250 billion entered the stock market during the first nine months of 1999. This fresh cash was not distributed evenly across the stock market as a whole. Much of it was coming from inexperienced individual investors. Media fawning over the

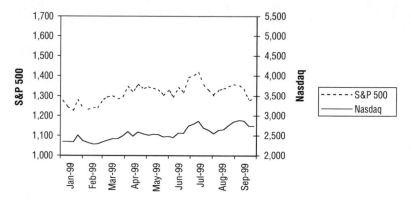

FIGURE 8.3   S&P 500 and Nasdaq, January 1999 to September 1999
Raw data obtained from Yahoo! Finance.

"new era" encouraged many of them to concentrate their holdings in technology stocks. For example, the largest technology mutual fund at the time, T. Rowe Price Science & Technology, ballooned to a whopping $12 billion in assets by the end of 1999. For comparison, the largest equity mutual fund at the time, Fidelity's Magellan Fund, had $106 billion in assets. In other words, a sector fund had accumulated nearly one-ninth the assets of the largest equity mutual fund! The T. Rowe Price Science & Technology fund's 42 percent return in 1998 and the 101 percent return in 1999 probably had more than a little to do with these massive inflows. With such fabulous returns in the technology sector, it is not surprising that the Nasdaq rose six times faster than the S&P 500 as the herd piled into shares of technology darlings.

Meanwhile, two other liquidity indicators were flashing yellow caution signals. During the first nine months of 1999, foreigners pumped $93 billion into U.S. stocks, an average of $10 billion per month. Inflows from foreigners occurred every month, just as one would expect as the U.S. stock market roared ahead. Also, investors were borrowing money to buy stocks at an alarming rate. Margin debt at NYSE member firms surged by $38 billion, or 27 percent, during the first nine months of 1999. Heavy foreign inflows and strong increases in margin debt are always bearish signals.

During this heady period, however, we were generally bullish on the stock market. We did recognize that a bubble was developing, but corporate buying, mutual fund inflows, and borrowed money were fueling the market's ascent. We were content to ride the bull market upward, although we recognized that favorable liquidity would not last forever. Our stance changed once the technology frenzy reached fever pitch at the end of 1999.

THE FRENZY: OCTOBER 1999 TO APRIL 2000

Liquidity indicators were not the only signs of increasing bullishness. A scan of business titles published in late 1999 would have been sufficient to raise the hackles of any contrarian. In June 1999, David Elias predicted in *Dow 40,000: Strategies for Profiting from the Greatest Bull Market in History* (McGraw-Hill) that the virtues of the "new economy" would lift the Dow Jones Industrial Average to 40,000 by 2016. Two other wildly bullish titles followed a few months later. In September 1999, Charles W. Kadlec's *Dow 100,000: Fact or Fiction* (New York Institute of Finance) appeared. According to the author, higher than normal economic growth and low inflation would lift the Dow to 100,000 by 2020. Finally, the infamous *Dow 36,000: The New Strategy for Profiting from the Coming Rise in the Stock Market*, by James Glassman and Kevin Hassett (Times Business), hit bookstores in October 1999. It argued stocks had been unreasonably undervalued for decades. The authors' "perfectly reasonable price" valuation measure suggested the Dow ought to trade around 36,000.

At this point, we should probably step back from these bubbly prognosticators and review the liquidity definition of a bubble. According to liquidity theory, a bubble forms when L2 and L3 continue to surge even after L1 has risen significantly. In other words, even after the house has become a heavy net seller, the players make sure they get fully invested before the market tops out. As we will see, this scenario is exactly what unfolded from October 1999 to April 2000, when the technology mania peaked.

From a close of 2,746.16 on September 30, 1999, the Nasdaq rocketed to its all-time record close of 5,048.62 on March 10, 2000, a gain of 84 percent in just five and a half months. (See Figure 8.4.) The beginning of the long ride down was just as steep. At the close on April 28, 2000, just one and a half months later, the Nasdaq had already fallen to 3,860.66, 24 percent below its all-time closing high. Even after this haircut in March and April, the Nasdaq still had risen 41 percent since October 1999. For comparison, the S&P 500 did not rise anywhere near as much as the Nasdaq. From the close of 1,282.71 on September 30, 1999, the S&P 500 closed at 1,452.43 on April 28, 2000, a gain of 13 percent. The S&P 500 finished this period only 5 percent below its all-time record close of 1,527.46 on March 24, 2000. Yet the S&P 500's all-time high would not come until five months later.

At the height of the bubble, the house bought far less heavily than it did during the first nine months of 1999. From October 1999 to April 2000, new cash takeovers totaled $74 billion, an average of $11 billion per month. This monthly average was only half of the $22 billion monthly average of new cash takeovers from January 1999 to September

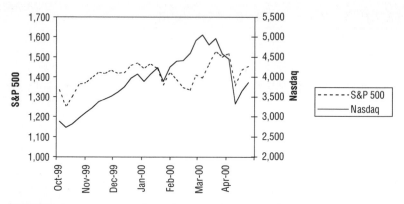

FIGURE 8.4   S&P 500 and Nasdaq, October 1999 to April 2000
Raw data obtained from Yahoo! Finance.

1999. On the other hand, new stock buybacks totaled $146 billion, an average of $21 billion per month. This monthly average was above the $14 billion monthly average of new stock buybacks from January 1999 to September 1999.

Not only was the house buying fewer shares in aggregate, it was pumping out more fresh paper than ever before. Remember, new offerings averaged $13 billion per month from January 1999 to September 1999. From October 1999 to April 2000, however, the house unloaded a staggering $179 billion in new shares, an average of $26 billion per month. Moreover, insider selling was surging as stock options began to unlock. In a year-end 1999 special report entitled "Why the Five Year Bull Market Is Ending," we estimated that over $800 billion of shares at year-end 1999 prices was waiting to unlock from IPOs in 1998 and 1999. The problem? As we will see, while inflows surged as the bubble reached its height, nowhere near $800 billion was available to satisfy the insiders who wished to unload their options at the top.

With corporate buying declining as new offerings and insider selling surged, corporate liquidity turned strongly bearish in November 1999. How did the market averages ascend to their all-time peaks? Individual investors were shoveling cash into the stock market at an unprecedented rate. From October 1999 to April 2000, investors pumped an astonishing $182 billion, or $26 billion per month, into U.S. equity funds. In February 2000, $37 billion gushed into U.S. equity funds, the highest monthly inflow ever. Not a single one of these seven months had a U.S. equity fund inflow below $15 billion. As Figure 8.5 shows, investors made sure they were fully invested right as the market topped out.

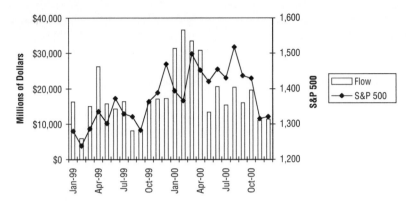

FIGURE 8.5 Monthly U.S. Equity Fund Flows versus S&P 500, January 1999 to December 2000
Source: Investment Company Institute, Yahoo! Finance.

Since we estimate that direct investment into U.S. equities equals U.S. equity fund flows, investors likely dumped at least $360 billion into U.S. equities in just seven months. Remember, this figure does not include all of the borrowed cash sending day trading favorites like Yahoo! and Juniper Networks into the stratosphere!

Two other indicators were flashing red warning signals even as the herd was flooding the stock market casino with cash. First, foreigners were snapping up U.S. stocks at an unprecedented rate. From October 1999 to April 2000, foreigners purchased $102 billion in U.S. stocks, an average of $15 billion per month. In February and March alone, foreigners bought $28 billion and $24 billion, respectively. As usual, heavy foreign buying coincided with the top of the market. Second, investors were borrowing to buy at a frantic pace. If the S&P 500 gained more than 20 percent during each year from 1995 to 1999, so the thinking went, why not borrow money from brokerage firms and capture even greater returns? The greedy excess of the technology bubble was no more apparent than in margin debt levels. From October 1999 to March 2000, margin debt at NYSE member firms surged a whopping 55 percent before retreating 10 percent in April 2000 right after the Nasdaq topped out. Like foreign buying, margin debt reached all-time record levels in February and March, hitting $265 billion and $279 billion, respectively. As usual, borrowing reached a climax just as the stock market did.

To summarize, the bubble formed as inflows and margin debt continued to surge even though the house had became a net seller. L1 began to rise in November 1999, four months before the Nasdaq peaked, primarily because of surging new offerings and insider selling. For a while, the tremendous surge of cash into the stock market casino—a good proportion of which was borrowed—sustained the market's advances. Many investors adopted the "greater fool" theory of investing. They continued to buy shares selling at grossly inflated prices because they felt confident they could always unload them to someone else who would be willing to pay higher prices. The stock market casino was a sure bet! By March 2000, however, nearly everyone was "all-in," and inflows did not surge any further. Nevertheless, the house was selling as heavily as ever, rushing to unload as many shares as the suckers were willing to buy. The result was one of the longest bear markets in stock market history.

THE BEGINNING OF THE LONG RIDE DOWN: MAY 2000 TO DECEMBER 2000

The stock market's indigestion was only beginning in April 2000. For the rest of the year, the Nasdaq continued on a relentless downward course. (See Figure 8.6.) From the close on April 28, 2000, to the close on December 29, 2000, the Nasdaq plummeted 36 percent from 3,860.66 to 2,470.52. The S&P 500 reached an all-time high of 1,530.01 during the day on September 1, 2000. From the close on April 28, 2000, to the close on December 29, 2000, the S&P 500 dropped from 1,452.43 to 1,320.28, a loss of 9 percent. The bubble had begun to burst.

The major averages headed south in late 2000 for three main reasons. First, the house remained a net seller even though corporate buying contin-

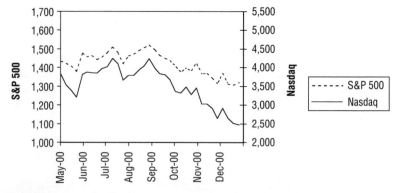

FIGURE 8.6   S&P 500 and Nasdaq, May 2000 to December 2000
Raw data obtained from Yahoo! Finance.

ued at a fairly robust pace. From May to December, new cash takeovers reached $184 billion, an average of $23 billion per month. Somewhat surprisingly, this monthly average was higher than the monthly averages of the previous two periods. At the same time, stock buybacks were announced totaling $106 billion, an average of $13 billion per month, which is roughly in line with the monthly averages of the previous two periods. Despite relatively high levels of corporate buying, however, corporate America remained a net seller. From May to December, the house sold $122 billion, or $15 billion per month, in fresh paper. This monthly average was well below the $26 billion monthly average from October 1999 to April 2000 and was roughly in line with the $13 billion monthly average from January 1999 to September 1999. What really surged during the last eight months of 2000 was insider selling. Major shareholders, top executives, and ordinary employees alike cashed out unlocking stock options at an unprecedented pace. During 2000, insiders sold $268 billion of their own companies' shares, an average of $22 billion per month. This rate of insider selling was double the monthly average of $11 billion that insiders sold in 1999. The flood of insider selling was more than enough to make up for the decline in new offerings and turn liquidity bearish.

Declining inflows into U.S. equities were the second reason the market declined. To be sure, inflows hardly dried up. From May to December, investors dumped $127 billion, an average of $16 billion per month, into U.S. equity funds. In fact, U.S. equity fund inflows never fell below $10 billion monthly during this period. Yet this pace was a decline from the $19 billion monthly average at the height of the bubble from October 1999 to April 2000, and inflows declined as 2000 drew to a close. Foreigners were the last to realize the party was over. From May to December, they bought $110 billion, an average of $14 billion per month, which was nearly equal to the monthly average at the height of the bubble. Clearly both U.S. and foreign investors hoped the glory days of early 2000 would return once the storm passed, even though the Nasdaq's sharp losses and the S&P 500's declines were beginning to challenge this optimistic forecast. Blissfully unaware that the house had already become a net seller, investors were net buyers of equities at the top. Many would curse their poor timing just a few years later.

The third reason for the market decline in late 2000 was the sharp decline in margin debt, which had fueled the rise of the technology darlings. What is astonishing, however, is how margin debt levels at NYSE member firms remained so high for so long. At the end of April, margin debt stood at $252 billion. During the following four months, it fell only slightly, and by September, it rose again to $251 billion. In other words, even though the Nasdaq had cratered 28 percent from its all-time high by the end of

September, margin debt levels remained nearly unchanged from April! Only in the fourth quarter of 2000 did investors curtail their use of margin debt. During this period, margin debt dropped 21 percent to $199 billion from $251 billion.

We should stress that inflows and margin debt levels, even by December 2000, were quite high. Yet they were not nearly high enough to offset all of the shares corporate America was unloading through new offerings and insider selling. Throughout most of 1999, the house and players were both net buyers. In late 1999 and early 2000, the house became a net seller, while the players were still buying heavily. In late 2000, the house continued selling, but the players were no longer buying nearly as heavily. The bubble had begun to burst, and the pain would get worse in the years ahead.

CHAPTER 9

The Aftermath

The aftermath of the technology bubble played out for three years after the Nasdaq peaked. Despite aggressive interest rate cuts by the Federal Reserve, the economy suffered a shallow recession in 2001. The September 11 terrorist attacks in New York and Washington, D.C., only compounded the nation's economic problems. These were difficult years for most investors, but not for followers of liquidity theory. By tracking the actions of the house and the players in the stock market casino, we were able to exploit the volatility of this period despite stock market weakness that persisted until March 2003.

2001: THE LONG RIDE DOWN CONTINUES

The year 2001 was not kind to the bulls, particularly those who were heavily committed to technology stocks. (See Figure 9.1.) After plunging 39 percent in 2000, the Nasdaq fell 21 percent in 2001, ending the year at 1,950.40. The S&P 500 suffered far milder declines. After falling 10 percent in 2000, the S&P 500 shed 13 percent in 2001, closing the year at 1,148.08. Shortly after the September 11 attacks, the losses on both indexes were much worse. The Nasdaq touched an intraday low of 1,418.15, while the S&P 500 touched an intraday low of 944.75.

The Market

Corporate liquidity was the key factor in the market's decline in 2001. While L1 rose a bearish $73 billion in 2000, it surged a whopping $261 billion in 2001, an average of $22 billion per month. In no other year has corporate liquidity been so heavily bearish. What drove this increase? First, new cash takeovers fell to a pace far below that of 1999 and 2000. During 2001, $94 billion in new cash takeovers was announced, a

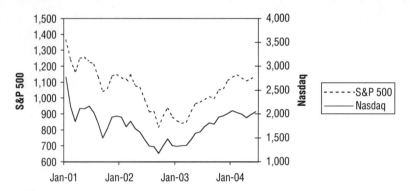

FIGURE 9.1 S&P 500 and Nasdaq, January 2001 to June 2004
Raw data obtained from Yahoo! Finance.

monthly pace of only $8 billion. This level of activity was a far cry from the $19 billion monthly pace in 1999 and the $20 billion monthly pace in 2000. As usual, the house saw the coming downturn well before the players. As a result, the house became far less inclined to use cash to buy other companies.

Meanwhile, the house unloaded even more new shares through new offerings and insider selling in 2001 than it had during the bubble years. New offerings reached an all-time record high of $317 billion, an average of $26 billion per month. This level of new offerings was substantially higher than the $15 billion monthly pace in 1999 and the $22 billion monthly pace in 2000. Like new offerings, insider selling reached an all-time record high as insiders rushed to cash out unlocking stock options while the window of opportunity remained open. Insiders dumped $293 billion in their own companies' shares, an average of $24 billion per month. This level of insider selling was well above the $11 billion monthly pace in 1999 and slightly higher than the $22 billion monthly pace in 2000.

New stock buybacks reached an all-time record of $238 billion, an average of $20 billion per month, in 2001. This pace compares quite favorably with the monthly averages of $15 billion in 1999 and $18 billion in 2000. A closer look at the data, however, reveals that it is not as bullish as it might appear. Nearly half of the annual total was announced following the September 11 attacks, and nearly a quarter of the annual total was announced in September alone, when stock prices reached their lowest levels of the entire year. As usual, the house was buying eagerly when the stock market was melting down and the players were panicking. In sum, the slightly higher level of new stock buybacks was nowhere near enough to compensate for the dramatic decline in new cash takeovers and increased levels of new offerings and insider selling. The house had become a big-time net seller.

Unfortunately for those long stocks, the players joined the house in reducing their purchases of U.S. equities. To be sure, the players were not net sellers like the house. In 2001, U.S. equity funds received $54 billion in fresh cash. Yet this inflow was nowhere near the massive $176 billion inflow in 1999 and the staggering $260 billion inflow in 2000. The players' feeble appetite for equities was apparent early in the year. In March 2001, U.S. equity funds posted a net outflow for the first time since August 1998. This outflow was the first of three monthly outflows from U.S. equity funds in 2001. At the same time, margin debt levels fell 24 percent from $199 billion at the end of 2000 to $150 billion at the end of 2001. The unwinding of the technology bubble made investors far less willing to borrow money to buy stocks.

The September 11 Terrorist Attacks

Before we discuss how we navigated the stock market in 2001, we want to highlight the aftermath of the September 11 terrorist attacks. Perhaps no other period provides greater insight into the contrasting responses of the house and the players to an exogenous shock. After the attacks, U.S. stock markets did not reopen until September 17. By the close on September 21, the S&P 500 had dropped 12 percent from its close on September 10. Over the same period, the Nasdaq cratered 16 percent. The reason for these steep declines? The players—institutions as well as individuals—panicked at the prospects of further terrorist attacks and promptly dumped stocks. In September 2001, U.S. equity funds experienced their worst one-month outflow ever up to that time—$27 billion—and investors probably yanked at least that much from U.S. stocks directly. What was the house doing during the panic? It was buying all of the shares the players were dumping! In September 2001, $54 billion in new stocks buybacks was announced, the most ever announced in a single month. While the players were panicking and dumping a record amount of U.S. equity fund shares, the house was buying back a record amount of shares!

What occurred during the last three months of 2001 is equally instructive. Rallying from its closing low of 965.80 on September 21, the S&P 500 climbed 19 percent to 1,148.08 by the close on December 31. Similarly, the Nasdaq jumped 37 percent from its closing low of 1,423.19 on September 21 to 1,950.40 by the close on December 31. These heady gains did not occur because the players decided to buy again. In fact, U.S. equity fund inflows totaled only $25 billion during the fourth quarter of 2001, and this $8 billion average monthly inflow was only slightly higher than the $7 billion average monthly inflow during the first eight months of the year. So what drove the rally? As the players were panicking about the possibility of further acts of terrorism, corporate buying accelerated. New stock buybacks averaged $21 billion per month during the fourth quarter, well above the average of $15 billion per month during the first eight months of the year. Clearly the house saw an opportunity to take advantage of falling stock prices in the aftermath of the September 11 attacks. Yet other liquidity indicators suggested the gains would be fleeting. New cash takeovers averaged only $4 billion per month during the fourth quarter, compared to an average of $9 billion per month during the first eight months of the year. And as stock prices rose, the house began selling fresh paper with extraordinary speed. While only $7 billion in new offerings were sold in September 2001—the lowest monthly total of the year—new offerings averaged $29 billion per month during the fourth quarter, which was slightly above the $28 billion monthly average during the first eight months of the year. The speed with which the new offering calendar resumed its torrid pace after the September sell-off was not a good omen.

How We Performed

Our model futures portfolio posted a 23 percent gain in 2001, trouncing the S&P 500, which lost 13 percent, and the Nasdaq, which lost 21 percent. We outperformed the major averages mainly because we followed the signals of corporate liquidity and assumed a bearish stance during most of the year. While we began the year bullish to ride the usual wave of fresh cash entering the market in January, we turned bearish in early February due to extremely heavy levels of new offerings and insider selling. We shifted between bullish and bearish stances from the end of February through the end of May, when we turned bearish. With only a few exceptions, we remained bearish until early September because corporate America was a heavy net seller. After the market reopened after the September 11 attacks and corporate buying exploded, we turned bullish until the end of September. In early October, however, we resumed our bearish stance because corporate buying began to slow and new offerings began to flood the market. Although the market continued to rise through November, we doubled our short position in early December. We realized the pension fund rebalancing that had driven stocks higher in November would be finished by December.

2002: THE BEAR DIGS IN

The year 2002 began with the September 11 attacks still fresh in America's memory. The S&P 500 and the Nasdaq had declined for two straight years. Surely, many investors thought, 2002 would be the year the stock market returned to its winning ways. The Nasdaq had plunged 39 percent in 2000 and 21 percent in 2001. How could things get any worse?

Investors were about to find out. During 2002, the Nasdaq dropped 32 percent. The S&P 500, which had been spared the worst of the carnage in 2000 and 2001, plunged 23 percent. At their lowest closes of the year on October 9, 2002—1,114.11 for the Nasdaq and 776.76 for the S&P 500— these two indexes were 78 percent and 49 percent below their all-time closing highs, respectively.

The Market

Followers of liquidity theory were fully aware of the reasons for the carnage: The house continued to be a net seller during the first half of the year even as inflows from individuals dried up. In 2002, L1 rose $87 billion. While this annual total was far below the $261 billion increase in 2001, it was still the second most bearish reading since the stock market boom of the 1990s began. While new offerings declined 38 percent to $198 billion in 2002 from $317 billion in 2001 and insider selling declined 73 percent to $79 billion in 2002 from $293 billion in 2001, corporate buying declined, too. New cash takeovers were consistently low all year. The annual total of $36 billion was 62 percent below the $94 billion announced in 2001 and the lowest annual total since we began tracking new cash takeovers in 1995. New stock buybacks also fell to $149 billion, a 37 percent decline from the $238 billion announced in 2001 and the lowest annual total since 1998. At the same time, the players were net sellers for the first time since the 1990s boom began, with U.S. equity funds suffering an annual outflow of $25 billion. Margin debt fell by $16 billion, its third consecutive annual decline. Finally, foreigners bought just $47 billion of U.S. stocks, the lowest annual total since 1996. With liquidity conditions so unfavorable, no wonder the major averages tanked.

To understand liquidity trends in 2002, it is necessary to divide the year in half. While the players were net buyers during the first five months of the year and net sellers during six of the last seven months of the year, the house was a net seller during the first six months of the year and a net buyer during five of the last six months of the year. As Figure 9.2 shows, when L1 rises as the house becomes more bearish, L2 almost always rises along with it as the players become more bullish. Conversely, when L1 falls

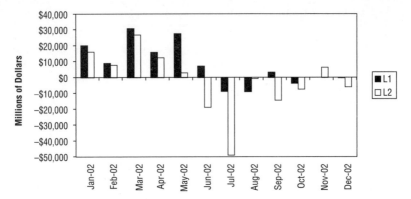

FIGURE 9.2 Monthly Corporate Liquidity (L1) versus Monthly U.S. Equity Fund Flows (L2), January 2002 to December 2002
Source: TrimTabs Investment Research, Investment Company Institute.

as the house becomes more bullish, L2 almost always falls along with it as the players become more bearish. Is it any wonder the house makes far more money in the stock market casino?

From January to June, L1 rose an average of $18 billion per month. The main reason for this surge was the new offering calendar. It averaged a whopping $24 billion per month, and it never dipped below $19 billion per month. At the same time, new cash takeovers and net stock buybacks were at low levels, averaging $3 billion per month and $10 billion per month, respectively. Not surprisingly, the S&P 500 shed 14 percent and the Nasdaq lost 25 percent during the first six months of 2002. The market's decline prompted the players to fold beginning in June, when U.S. equity funds suffered a $19 billion outflow, their first monthly outflow since the $27 billion outflow in September 2001. Until June, the players had been pumping an average of $13 billion per month into U.S. equity funds even as the house was selling heavily.

The stock market reached two major bottoms in 2002, one in late July and the other in early October. During the summer, the major indexes each experienced waterfall-type declines. By July 23, the S&P 500 closed at a near-term bottom of 797.70. A few weeks later, on August 5, the Nasdaq closed at a near-term bottom of 1,206.01. The market staged a feeble recovery attempt in August and September, but it dropped again in October. The bottom of the bear market finally arrived on October 9, 2002, with the S&P 500 at 776.76 and the Nasdaq at 1,114.11.

With stocks on sale, did the players decide to stock up? Certainly not! U.S. equity funds posted outflows during all but one month from June to

December, and the average monthly outflow during these seven months was a hefty $13 billion. Not surprisingly, selling reached its height in July, when the S&P 500 was just 20 points from its ultimate closing bottom. A staggering $49 billion left U.S. equity funds that month, the largest monthly U.S equity fund outflow ever. U.S. equity fund outflows also reached $14 billion in September and $7 billion in October, and the market reached its ultimate closing bottom in early October. The players had little interest in buying when stock prices were low.

On the other hand, the house had different ideas. From June to December, L1 declined by an average of $3 billion per month. While this level of corporate buying is hardly robust, it was enough to ensure that the lows reached by the S&P 500 and the Nasdaq in early October were not a great deal lower than those they had reached during late July and early August. In fact, the S&P 500 and the Nasdaq finished the year 13 percent and 20 percent, respectively, above their October 9 closing lows. The worst of the bear market had passed.

How We Performed

Our model futures portfolio posted a 74 percent gain in 2002, leaving the S&P 500 and the Nasdaq in the dust. We dramatically outperformed the major averages mainly because we followed the actions of the house. When the house was bearish during the first half of the year, we were bearish. When the house turned more bullish during the second half of the year, we turned more bullish, too.

Our model futures portfolio began the year bearish. Except for a brief foray into a small long position from late February to early March, we maintained our bearish stance until the end of June due to the predominance of corporate selling. At that point, we turned neutral for two reasons. First, new offerings and insider selling began to slow. Second, U.S. equity funds posted a heavy outflow of $19 billion in June. Such a large outflow often marks a bottom. Meanwhile, corporate buying was beginning to increase. Unfortunately we turned cautiously bullish in early July, which was two weeks too soon. Nevertheless, corporate buying spiked in July, and new offerings nearly ground to a halt in August while individual investors were panicking.

We remained bullish until early September. Then we turned bearish because corporate buying abruptly stopped. In mid-October, we turned cautiously bullish due to a pickup in corporate buying. We shifted between bullish and bearish positions from mid-October until mid-December, when we turned bullish. Corporate buying was beginning to resume, and new offerings and insider selling were slowing, as they typically do at the end of the year. More importantly, we expected corporate America to pump as much as $100 billion into pension funds at the beginning of 2003 due to the stock market losses of the previous two years. As we discuss in the next section, pension funds were not the only investors pumping money into the U.S. stock market in early 2003.

2003: THE BULL RETURNS

There was little cheer on Wall Street or Main Street at the end of 2002. Sentiment among investors was about as bearish as we have ever seen it. Pundits were openly wondering whether the markets would suffer a fourth straight year of declines. Business titles released in late 2002 certainly reflected the prevailing mood. Robert Prechter's *Conquer the Crash: You Can Survive and Prosper in a Deflationary Depression* (John Wiley & Sons) appeared in June 2002. As the title suggests, Prechter believed the United States would soon be gripped by a deflationary depression. Daniel A. Arnold's *The Great Bust Ahead: The Greatest Depression in American and UK History Is Just Several Short Years Away* (InstantPublisher.com), which was published in December 2002, reached a similar conclusion. Arnold predicted that during the first quarter of the twenty-first century, perhaps as early as 2009–2010, America and Britain would suffer a depression far worse than what occurred during the 1930s. The authors of the "Rich Dad, Poor Dad" series also joined the pessimists. Robert T. Kiyosaki and Sharon L. Lechter's *Rich Dad's Prophecy: Why the Biggest Stock Market Crash in History Is Still Coming . . . and How You Can Prepare Yourself and Profit from It!* (Warner Books), published in October 2002, warned of a massive stock market crash once the first baby boomers celebrated their seventieth birthdays in 2016. While the past three years had been extremely painful for many investors, these books and others assured them things were going to get a whole lot worse.

The Market

During the first three months of 2003, investors' jitters proved somewhat justified. As investors fretted about the economic impact of the impending war with Iraq, the S&P 500 fell 4 percent, and the Nasdaq was nearly unchanged. Despite the prevailing pessimism, corporate America continued to be a net buyer during each of the first three months of the year, just as it had been during all but one month since July 2002. L1 declined an average of $6 billion per month. New cash takeovers remained low at an average of just $3 billion per month, but new stock buyback activity surged to a robust $17 billion per month, which compares favorably with the monthly averages of $20 billion in 2001 and $12 billion in 2002. At the same time, however, new offerings and insider selling were nowhere near the pace of the previous two years. New offerings averaged only $10 billion per month, compared to the monthly averages of $26 billion in 2001 and $16 billion in 2002. Insider selling declined to only $4 billion per month, compared to the monthly averages of $24 billion in 2001 and $7 billion in 2002. While the house was in a buying mood, however, the players continuing selling, yanking an average of $3 billion per month from U.S. equity funds.

On March 13, just two days after the stock market reached a third major bottom on March 11, Charles Biderman appeared on Bloomberg Television. He predicted that the overall stock market would pop 20 percent to 25 percent once investors realized the Iraq war would not be fought in the United States. This prediction turned out to be prescient. From the bottom on March 11 to the end of the year, the S&P 500 rose 39 percent, and the Nasdaq surged an astonishing 58 percent. A new bull market was born.

What drove these heady gains? It was definitely not corporate buying. Beginning in April, corporate America became a net seller, and it continued to be a net seller during every month for the rest of the year except December. From April to December, L1 surged an average of $11 billion per month. New cash takeovers, which had been unimpressive since early 2001, remained low at just $6 billion per month. New stock buybacks were stronger at $11 billion per month, although December accounted for 26 percent of the dollar amount during these nine months as corporations rushed to do something deemed positive before the holidays. On the other side of the corporate liquidity ledger, new offerings and insider selling exploded. From April to December, a whopping $170 billion in new offerings was sold, an average of $19 billion per month. To put this flood of fresh paper into perspective, an average of $26 billion per month in new offerings was sold during 2001, the heaviest year ever for new offerings. At the same time, insiders unloaded $83 billion of their own companies' shares, an average of $9 billion per month. The signals from the house were consistently bearish.

With corporate America as a net seller, inflows from individuals, pension funds, and hedge funds provided the fuel for the 2003 rally. This period serves as a perfect example of why followers of liquidity theory need to pay attention to both the house and the players. While corporate liquidity was bearish, the inflows from the players were enough to take the market higher, as Figure 9.3 demonstrates.

From April to December, investors pumped $139 billion, an average of $15 billion per month, into U.S. equity funds. In addition, margin debt at

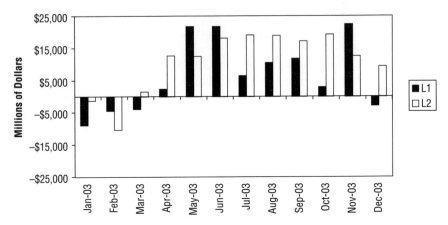

FIGURE 9.3   Monthly Corporate Liquidity (L1) versus Monthly U.S. Equity Fund
Flows (L2), January 2003 to December 2003
Source: TrimTabs Investment Research, Investment Company Institute.

NYSE member firms surged $33 billion, an average of $4 billion per
month. Euphoria over the supposedly painless end to the Iraq war drove
the players' increased appetite for equities. Yet it was not just individual investors who were buying heavily. Hedge funds that had entered the second
quarter of 2003 either net short or drastically underinvested shoveled at
least $200 billion into equities during the second quarter. Also, pension
fund sponsors—including municipalities—sold long-term bonds heavily
during the second quarter to buy stocks. Institutional money and individual inflows powered the market higher in 2003.

Liquidity theory defines a bubble as a period in which the market capitalization continues rising after the net float has surged. That is exactly
what occurred during the last nine months of 2003 in technology and
small-capitalization stocks. While L1 rose $99 billion from April to De-
cember, the market capitalization surged from $10.7 trillion to $15.3 trillion, a gain of 43 percent. As we discuss in the next section, the hangover
from the stock market party of 2003 was beginning.

How We Performed

We were admittedly less successful in 2003 than we had been in 2001 and
2002. While the S&P 500 rose 26 percent and the Nasdaq rose 50 percent,
our model portfolio lost 7 percent. The year began auspiciously enough.
We began the year bullish as corporate buying was fairly heavy. From mid-

January to the beginning of February, we turned short as corporate buying eased somewhat. Beginning in mid-February, as individual investors were panicking about the impact of the Iraq war, we turned cautiously bullish. We became increasingly bullish from the end of February to the beginning of April, gradually adding to our long positions. These proved to be profitable trades. By the end of April, our model portfolio had risen 9 percent for the year. At that point, we turned neutral, and we became increasingly bearish in April and May as corporate buying slowed and U.S. equity fund inflows surged. We were waiting for the new offering calendar to accelerate now that individual investors were dumping money into stocks.

Remaining short from the beginning of May to the end of October turned out to be a major mistake. We did not realize the decimation of Wall Street corporate finance departments during the summer of 2002 meant that not enough new offerings would debut to absorb all of the cash flooding into equities. We also did not realize hedge funds and pension funds would shift hundreds of billions of dollars into the stock market during the spring and that euphoria over the apparent quick and painless end to the Iraq war would keep individuals pumping new cash into the stock market over the summer. We finally turned bullish at the end of October and made back some of the year's losses during the last two months of the year. Our difficulties during the middle of 2003 were a humbling reminder that we need to be constantly vigilant for what we don't know we don't know about the financial markets.

EARLY 2004: THE BUBBLE DEFLATES

The market began to sputter in early 2004 as investors gradually lost their enthusiasm for equities and corporate buying remained fairly lackluster. By the end of June, the rally from the March 2003 lows looked tired. The S&P 500 reached a closing high of 1,157.76 on February 11. By the end of June, however, it closed at 1,125.38, only 1 percent higher than where it began the year. Similarly, the Nasdaq reached a closing high of 2,153.83 on January 26. By the end of June, it closed at 2,047.79, only 2 percent higher than where it began the year. The bubble, which was most concentrated in small-capitalization stocks and technology stocks, began to deflate.

The Market

What stopped the market's ascent? Corporate America continued to be a net seller. From January to June, L1 rose an average of $4 billion per month. Not counting Cingular's $41 billion takeover of AT&T Wireless,

L1 rose an average of $8 billion per month, which was equal to the monthly average in 2003. To be sure, corporate buying was not dormant. New cash takeovers averaged $14 billion per month ($4 billion per month without counting the AT&T Wireless deal), and new stock buybacks averaged $18 billion per month. Corporate liquidity was bearish mainly because of the extremely heavy new offering calendar. New offerings averaged $22 billion per month, and they never fell below $15 billion during any month. In other words, the house sold nearly as much fresh paper during the first six months of 2004 as it did during the first six months of 2000! Meanwhile, insider selling averaged a heavy $11 billion per month. Factoring out the liquidity impact of the AT&T Wireless deal, corporate buying was nowhere near a match for corporate selling.

Meanwhile, individual investors were losing their appetite for equities. U.S. equity funds attracted a whopping $82 billion in fresh cash during the first six months of 2004, an average of $14 billion per month. This total alone, however, presents a misleading picture of the actions of the players. U.S. equity fund flows declined from an inflow of $31 billion in January—the largest one-month inflow ever recorded—to a small outflow of $900 million in May before rebounding to an $8 billion inflow in June. Once the major averages peaked in January and February, individual investors became disillusioned with equities quite quickly.

Remember how we described the stock market in late 2003 and early 2004 as a bubble concentrated in technology and small-capitalization stocks? The bubble did deflate somewhat. The Nasdaq peaked at 2,153.83 on January 26 and bottomed at 1,876.64 on May 17, a decline of 13 percent. Similarly, the Russell 2000 peaked at 599.54 on March 5 and bottomed at 535.34 on May 17, a decline of 11 percent. This market action might not seem like much of a bubble burst. At the beginning of the year, we had expected these declines to be nearer 30 percent than 10 percent. The damage would have been much worse if the economy had not begun to grow as rapidly as it did during the first half of the year. From December 2003 to June 2004, personal income consistently rose at an annualized rate exceeding 5 percent. There is nothing like surging economic growth to relieve the pressure on investors who are overleveraged in risky stocks.

How We Performed

After a disappointing year in 2003, our performance dramatically improved during the first nine months of 2004. While the S&P 500 was nearly flat and the Nasdaq lost 5 percent, our model futures portfolio gained 11 percent.

We began the year bullish, as we had been since the end of October, primarily due to the flood of year-end bonus and retirement money flooding into the stock market in January. We remained bullish until the end of February, when U.S. equity fund inflows no longer bridged the gap between corporate buying and corporate selling. As a result, we turned bearish, and we remained bearish until mid-May. Not only were U.S. equity fund inflows far lower than they had been at the beginning of the year, but corporate buying was practically nonexistent. During the last week of April, however, we were surprised when corporate buying began to rebound, and we turned bullish in mid-May. It was one of the rare moments when we called the bottom precisely, as both the Nasdaq and the Russell 2000 bottomed on May 17. We remained bullish until the end of June, when we turned bearish due to rising corporate selling and declining corporate buying.

We alternated between cautiously bearish and cautiously bullish stances until mid-July, when we turned cautiously bullish. We remained cautiously bullish from mid-July until mid-August because corporate buying was respectable, and we expected new offerings to slow at the end of the summer. At the end of August, we turned fully bullish to take advantage of the new offering calendar's extended Labor Day vacation. As the new offering calendar gathered momentum in September, however, we tempered our bullishness. By the end of September, we turned cautiously bearish due to an explosion of new offerings and a slowdown in corporate buying.

Yet no matter what curves the market throws, liquidity theory can help investors navigate the road ahead. How do we know? The performance of our model futures portfolio speaks for itself. Since we began separating corporate buying and selling from equity inflows in our liquidity analysis in September 2000, our model futures portfolio has handily outperformed the S&P 500. From September 2000 through December 2004, our model futures portfolio gained 115 percent, while the S&P 500 declined 16 percent. Tracking the actions of the house and the players in the stock market casino has proven to be quite profitable, even during one of the most tumultuous periods in the history of the U.S. financial markets.

Liquidity Theory
in Action

Swinging for Singles: Lower-Risk Strategies

While Part Two is devoted to the past, Part Three focuses squarely on the present. Specifically, it outlines a series of liquidity-based investment strategies you can use to manage your own portfolio. While much of this material is geared toward individual investors, institutional investors can also deploy the strategies we outline in their portfolios on a larger scale with different products.

In this chapter, we discuss our general investment approach and four lower-risk investment strategies. As mentioned in Chapter 1, the strategies we present in this book are designed for people who want to manage their portfolios in a professional manner. If you have no interest in learning about investments and monitoring financial markets and you want to invest for long-term goals, we recommend you simply dollar-cost average into a diversified portfolio of Vanguard index funds. The strategies we outline in this chapter are not particularly complex, but you should be thoroughly familiar with how the stock market casino operates before you use them.

INVESTMENT APPROACH

This book makes no pretense of being a comprehensive guide to investment management. It discusses only how to handle assets placed at risk in the stock market. Other important considerations for individual investors—including cash savings, insurance, and real estate—receive no treatment in this book.

We begin by stressing an obvious but often neglected point: There is no one right investment strategy for all investors. A $2 billion hedge fund will invest far differently than a young couple with two small children, who will in turn invest differently than an octogenarian widower.

Nevertheless, we believe two main factors should guide all investors as they develop their strategies:

1. *Time horizon.* How far away are the goals for which you are investing? Are you investing money you intend to use as a down payment on a home in a few years? Or are you saving for a retirement that is at least 30 years away? In general, the shorter your time horizon, the less risk you should assume in your portfolio. We do not recommend investing money you may need within 10 years in equities because of their volatility over shorter time periods.
2. *Attitude toward risk.* How you behaved in the past is a generally reliable guide to how you will behave in the future. On the one hand, if you panicked during the 2000–2002 bear market and shifted your equity investments into bonds or cash, you should probably use a conservative investment strategy. On the other hand, if you scooped up stocks with both hands while the herd panicked during the bear market bottoms of July 2002, October 2002, and March 2003, you can probably afford to assume more risk in your portfolio. Life is too short to worry constantly about your investments. Choose an investment strategy that allows you to sleep comfortably at night.

Note that we have yet to mention anything about investment returns. While every investor dreams of handsome returns, you should focus on risks rather than returns as you design and manage your portfolio. While higher-risk strategies may offer higher returns, they will not do you any good if you abandon them when the inevitable difficult periods come.

Liquidity theory is a macro timing tool. Thus, our strategies exclusively use indexed equity products—including index mutual funds, index exchange-traded funds (ETFs), and stock index futures. We make no attempt to select individual stocks or market sectors. We also do not use actively managed equity mutual funds or hedge funds in our strategies because we believe fewer than 200 investment managers of any type can consistently beat the stock market averages after expenses. While exceptional managers do exist, it is extremely difficult to identify them in advance. Moreover, many of the best managers do not accept new money because they realize bigger is not always better in the investment management game. Outside of equities, we use short-term bond index mutual funds and short-term bond index ETFs in our strategies. We believe short-term bonds are the best tool to reduce risk in a portfolio. Short-term bonds offer higher returns than cash equivalents with only marginally more risk. We steer clear of long-term bonds. The historical long-term returns of long-term bonds do not justify their considerable interest rate risks. We also steer clear of junk bonds, which behave far more like stocks than bonds. Finally, we avoid active bond management because we do not believe it is worth the additional risk and expenses.

In our strategies, we vary our contributions and holdings according to expected liquidity conditions. Since we want to invest on the side of the house in the stock market casino, we adopt one of five stances depending on our estimates of the net change in the trading float of shares (L1) for the coming week. (See Table 10.1).

For example, if we estimated that corporate America would be a net buyer of $500 million daily, then we would be bullish. If we estimated that corporate America would be a net seller of $900 million daily, then we would be strongly bearish. Of course, sometimes we modify our liquidity stances based on what we expect the players in the stock market casino to do. For example, if we expected extremely heavy U.S. equity fund inflows during a week when we expected L1 to be cautiously bearish, we might turn neutral or even cautiously bullish rather than cautiously bearish. Remember, liquidity theory is partly an art and partly a science.

The first two strategies in this chapter use Vanguard index mutual funds. These funds have low expense ratios and no sales loads, which allow investors to keep a greater percentage of their investment returns. Also, Vanguard's chief investment officer, George U. "Gus" Sauter, oversees all of Vanguard's index funds. While many people assume almost anyone can run an index fund, effective management of an index fund requires considerable transactional skill, and Sauter's team is one of the best index fund managers in the business. In fact, Vanguard's 500 Index fund, the second-largest mutual fund in the world, often manages to beat the S&P 500 slightly because of astute trading techniques.

Vanguard is a fine company with which to invest, but other alternatives are equally suited to liquidity-based strategies, particularly for in-

TABLE 10.1 Liquidity Stances

Daily L1	Stance
<–$800 million	Strongly bullish
–$400 million to –$800 million	Bullish
–$400 million to $400 million	Neutral
$400 million to $800 million	Bearish
>$800 million	Strongly bearish

vestors who wish to trade their existing holdings or use leverage. For individual investors, many investment companies—including Fidelity, T. Rowe Price, Charles Schwab, and TIAA-CREF—offer low-cost index funds that can be purchased directly or through a discount broker. Many individual and institutional investors are increasingly using ETFs offered by companies such as Barclays Global Investors and State Street Global Advisors. Like mutual funds, ETFs have no sales loads and low expense ratios, and they provide broad diversification. Unlike mutual funds, however, ETFs can be bought and sold like stocks anytime during the day. While this feature offers investors greater flexibility, it also requires paying a brokerage commission each time ETF shares are bought and sold. Finally, institutional investors have access to a wide variety of sophisticated investment options—including stock index futures—to implement their investment strategies.

None of the examples in this chapter uses leverage, or borrowed money, because we do not consider any strategy involving borrowed money to be a low-risk strategy. Except for highly experienced individual investors, the use of leverage is best left to professionals. Many people dream about the alluring returns that are possible by using borrowed money. After all, borrowing 100 percent of a portfolio's value to invest in an index product that increases 20 percent in one year provides a return of 40 percent on the portfolio's value (excluding the interest cost of the borrowed capital). Unfortunately the opposite is also true: If the index product declines by 20 percent in one year, a loss would result equal to 40 percent of portfolio's value, excluding the interest cost of the borrowed capital.

With these preliminaries aside, it's time to put liquidity theory into action! We begin with our most conservative strategy and work through more aggressive strategies.

Dollar-Cost Averaging

Timed contributions: Yes

Trading: No

Short positions: No

Leverage: No

Our first strategy is highly conservative. It is designed for investors who wish to time their regular purchases but who do not wish to trade their existing holdings, establish short positions, or use leverage. This strategy requires attention only once a month, so it is ideal for investors who are unable or unwilling to spend the time necessary to adjust to market conditions on a weekly basis. This strategy also works well for investors in taxable accounts, since it avoids generating the taxes and paperwork of trading in a taxable account.

Here is an example of how this strategy works. Karen is a single, 45-year-old attorney who expects to continue working well into her sixties. Karen wishes to hold about two-thirds of her existing individual retirement account (IRA), which has a value of $150,000, in stocks and about one-third in short-term bonds, although she is willing to deviate somewhat from these allocations when liquidity conditions warrant. She also wishes to add $300 to her IRA each month.

Since Karen will only time her purchases and will not trade her existing holdings, she can use Vanguard index mutual funds to construct her portfolio. For the stock portion of her portfolio, she chooses the Vanguard Total Stock Market Index Fund (VTSMX), which provides low-cost exposure to the entire U.S. stock market. For the bond portion of her portfolio, she chooses the Vanguard Short-Term Bond Index Fund (VBISX), which provides low-cost exposure to short-term Treasury, mortgage, and corporate bonds. Conventional dollar-cost averaging would dictate that regardless of market conditions, Karen should put $200 per month (67 percent of her monthly investment) into VTSMX and $100 per month (33 percent of her monthly investment) into VBISX. Even if an equity bubble formed and corporations were heavy net sellers, following a conventional dollar-cost averaging strategy would still dictate that she put 67 percent of her monthly investment into stocks. Similarly, even if a bear market had raged for years and corporations were heavy net buyers, a conventional dollar-cost averaging strategy would still dictate that she put 33 percent of her monthly investment into bonds.

Instead, Karen uses dollar-cost averaging in her IRA while still taking advantage of liquidity theory. Dollar-cost averaging according to liquidity theory means she buys proportionally more stocks the more the house is a net buyer and buys proportionally more bonds the more the house is a net seller. Karen initially establishes IRA accounts with Vanguard, placing $100,000 (two-thirds of the value of her existing IRA) into VTSMX and $50,000 (one-third of the value of her existing IRA) into VBISX. Then she contributes $300 to her portfolio each month—just like someone following a conventional dollar-cost averaging strategy—but the allocation of her monthly contribution varies each month depending on current liquidity conditions. (See Table 10.2.)

Using this conservative strategy, Karen buys proportionally more stocks when the house is buying and buys proportionally more bonds when the house is selling. Her returns should easily outstrip those of conventional dollar-cost averaging. Yet this strategy requires only one investment decision every month, which minimizes the time she needs to spend

TABLE 10.2 Dollar-Cost Averaging

Liquidity	VTSMX	VBISX
Strongly bullish	$300 (100%)	$0 (0%)
Bullish	$200 (67%)	$100 (33%)
Neutral	$150 (50%)	$150 (50%)
Bearish	$100 (33%)	$200 (67%)
Strongly bearish	$0 (0%)	$300 (100%)

planning her investments. She appreciates this low-maintenance approach because it allows her to focus her energies on her career and her other interests rather than the stock market. It also minimizes her risk, which is important to her because she knows she does not have a strong stomach for market volatility. Finally, if she chooses to maintain a relatively steady asset allocation between stocks and bonds, she can always rebalance her portfolio between stocks and bonds every year or so.

Enhanced Dollar-Cost Averaging

Timed contributions: Yes

Trading: No

Short positions: No

Leverage: No

Our next strategy is a slightly more adventurous variation of the dollar-cost averaging strategy just described. It works in much the same way, except it adds a small-capitalization stock index fund and tilts the allocation percentages more heavily toward stocks.

Ryan graduated from Duke University with a degree in architecture three years ago. After graduation, he landed his first job at a top commercial design firm in Atlanta. Ryan has paid off his student loans, built up some cash for an emergency fund, and has $3,000 accumulated in a Vanguard 500 Index Roth IRA account. Living on an entry-level salary in a relatively expensive area, he has only $4,000 to invest each year. He wisely decides to funnel this money into his Roth IRA, contributing $400 per month during each of the first 10 months of the year. Unlike Karen, Ryan does not care if he deviates from a fixed asset allocation—he is willing to put his fresh cash wherever liquidity theory dictates—but he does want to dollar-cost average into his Roth IRA every month. He is not comfortable

TABLE 10.3   Enhanced Dollar-Cost Averaging

Liquidity	NAESX	VFINX	VBISX
Strongly bullish	$200 (50%)	$200 (50%)	$0 (0%)
Bullish	$120 (30%)	$280 (70%)	$0 (0%)
Neutral	$0 (0%)	$200 (50%)	$200 (50%)
Bearish	$0 (0%)	$160 (40%)	$240 (60%)
Strongly bearish	$0 (0%)	$120 (30%)	$280 (70%)

with trading his holdings, going short, or using leverage. Finally, since he is only 24 years old and is comfortable with some additional risk, he wants to tilt his allocations slightly more toward stocks than he might otherwise do if he were older.

To implement an enhanced dollar-cost averaging strategy, Ryan uses three Vanguard no-load mutual funds: Vanguard Small-Cap Index Fund (NAESX), Vanguard 500 Index Fund (VFINX), and Vanguard Short-Term Bond Index Fund (VBISX). To begin, he divides the $3,000 in his existing VFINX Roth IRA account equally among three Roth IRA accounts in NAESX, VFINX, and VBISX. This arrangement satisfies the $1,000 minimum investment required for a Roth IRA account in each of these funds. Then he dollar-cost averages $400 into his Roth IRA accounts during the first 10 months of the year according to liquidity conditions. (See Table 10.3.)

While this approach restricts itself to dollar-cost averaging, the small-cap fund and the percentage allocations make this strategy more aggressive than Karen's. Note that Ryan uses the NAESX, which holds small-capitalization stocks, to boost returns during bullish and strongly bullish periods. Note, too, that even during bearish and strongly bearish periods, he still invests 40 percent and 30 percent, respectively, into VFINX. By introducing small-cap stocks and higher stock allocations, this strategy does involve greater risk. But since Ryan is 30 or 40 years from retirement, he decides the potential rewards outweigh the extra risk.

Split Portfolio

Timed contributions: Yes

Trading: Yes

Short positions: No

Leverage: No

Our third strategy moves beyond dollar-cost averaging. It is designed for investors who wish to trade some of their existing holdings as well as time their investments of fresh cash. This strategy is ideal for investors who are willing to assume greater risks in their portfolio but do not wish to go short or use leverage. It requires somewhat more time to manage than the two dollar cost-averaging strategies, but it also offers the potential for greater rewards. It works particularly well for investors who have assets divided between taxable accounts and nontaxable retirement accounts, since the trading in this strategy is completed in nontaxable retirement accounts to avoid tax consequences.

Terry and Michael are a couple in their mid-40s with two young children. Terry is a stay-at-home mother, and Michael is a sales manager for a payroll services firm. Michael also operates a small remodeling business to generate extra income. Michael is comfortable with equities, but Terry has always preferred more secure but lower-yielding investments like money market funds, bank certificates of deposit, and bonds. They can afford to invest $500 per month in their taxable accounts, $4,000 per year in each of their Roth IRA accounts, and $5,000 per year in Michael's SIMPLE-IRA account. In designing their investment portfolio, the couple decides to compromise. To satisfy Terry, they decide to hold their taxable accounts in index mutual funds in which they do not trade, go short, or use leverage. In their taxable accounts, they use liquidity theory to allocate contributions of fresh cash. At the same time, however, Terry and Michael each have a Roth IRA account they established years ago. Michael also has a SIMPLE-IRA, which he funds with income from his sideline business. The couple decides they will trade their retirement accounts according to liquidity conditions.

In their taxable portfolio, they allocate 50 percent of their existing $50,000 holdings to the Vanguard Tax-Managed Growth and Income Fund (VTGIX), which tracks the S&P 500. They choose this fund instead of the Vanguard 500 Index Fund (VFINX) for their taxable portfolio. This fund tracks the S&P 500 while using various trading techniques to minimize capital gains, and they can afford this fund's $10,000 minimum initial investment. They allocate the other 50 percent of their existing holdings to the Vanguard Limited-Term Tax-Exempt Fund (VMLTX). This short-term bond fund is appropriate for investors like Terry and Michael who are in high federal income tax brackets. This allocation is relatively conservative, so Terry is satisfied. They follow the dollar-cost averaging technique outlined earlier, varying their monthly contribution of $500 according to current liquidity conditions. (See Table 10.4.) If they choose, they can rebalance their holdings every year or so to keep the 50 percent stock/50 percent bond allocation relatively fixed.

TABLE 10.4 Split Portfolio: Taxable Contributions

Liquidity	VTGIX	VMLTX
Strongly bullish	$500 (100%)	$0 (0%)
Bullish	$375 (75%)	$125 (25%)
Neutral	$250 (50%)	$250 (50%)
Bearish	$125 (25%)	$375 (75%)
Strongly bearish	$0 (0%)	$500 (100%)

The couple takes a more active approach in their retirement portfolio. They not only allocate fresh cash strategically, but they also trade their existing holdings. To execute this strategy, they elect to use Barclays Global Investors iShares ETFs in their Roth IRA and SIMPLE-IRA accounts at a discount broker. This arrangement offers them the flexibility to buy and sell without the trading restrictions many mutual fund companies impose. Trading in their retirement accounts also prevents them from incurring tax consequences from their trades.

They select three ETFs to implement their retirement portfolio strategy: the iShares S&P 500 Index (IVV), the iShares S&P SmallCap 600 Index (IJR), and the iShares Lehman 1–3 Year Treasury Bond Fund (SHY). They prefer to invest new money in their IRA accounts twice a year: $2,000 in January and $2,000 in July. Each January and July, they allocate their $2,000 contributions according to current liquidity conditions. (See Table 10.5.)

Michael follows the same strategy with his $1,250 contribution to his SIMPLE-IRA account each quarter, although the dollar amounts obviously differ because he is investing $1,250 rather than $2,000 at a time. Note that the couple's Roth IRAs are not tilted nearly as heavily toward stocks during neutral, bearish, or strongly bearish liquidity conditions as Ryan's Roth IRA. Since the couple is in their mid-40s, the time horizon for their

TABLE 10.5 Split Portfolio: Nontaxable Contributions

Liquidity	IJR	IVV	SHY
Strongly bullish	$1,000 (50%)	$1,000 (50%)	$0 (0%)
Bullish	$600 (30%)	$1,400 (70%)	$0 (0%)
Neutral	$0 (0%)	$800 (40%)	$1,200 (60%)
Bearish	$0 (0%)	$400 (20%)	$1,600 (80%)
Strongly bearish	$0 (0%)	$0 (0%)	$2,000 (100%)

TABLE 10.6   Split Portfolio: Nontaxable Holdings

Liquidity	IJR	IVV	SHY
Strongly bullish	$15,000 (50%)	$15,000 (50%)	$0 (0%)
Bullish	$9,000 (30%)	$21,000 (70%)	$0 (0%)
Neutral	$0 (0%)	$12,000 (40%)	$18,000 (60%)
Bearish	$0 (0%)	$6,000 (20%)	$24,000 (80%)
Strongly bearish	$0 (0%)	$0 (0%)	$30,000 (100%)

investments is shorter, so they pare back on stocks more quickly as liquidity deteriorates.

The couple also trades their existing holdings depending on liquidity conditions every month. Terry and Michael are busy raising two small children, so they do not feel they have the time to monitor liquidity more frequently. Also, they want to minimize trading expenses in their brokerage account. Currently they hold $30,000 in each Roth IRA account and $18,000 in Michael's SIMPLE-IRA account. They allocate their holdings in each Roth IRA account according to current liquidity conditions. (See Table 10.6.) Michael follows the same strategy with his SIMPLE-IRA account, although the dollar amounts obviously differ because his SIMPLE-IRA account holds $18,000 rather than $30,000.

Here is how their trading would work. Suppose liquidity is neutral during one month. In each Roth IRA account, the couple would hold $12,000 in IVV and $18,000 in SHY. If liquidity turned bearish the next month, the couple would sell $6,000 in shares from IVV and buy $6,000 in shares in SHY in each Roth IRA account. They feel comfortable with trading in their Roth IRA and SIMPLE-IRA accounts because doing so does not have tax consequences. Meanwhile, they do not trade any of the holdings in their taxable portfolio.

Long-Short Split Portfolio

Timed contributions: Yes

Trading: Yes

Short positions: Yes

Leverage: No

Our final strategy is much the same as the split portfolio, except it permits short positions of up to 100 percent in the nontaxable portfolio when liquidity is strongly bearish. Still, it is not aggressive because it does not use any leverage. Also, trading is restricted to the nontaxable portfolio. This strategy does not require much more time to manage than the split portfolio, but it does require comfort with the more substantial risks of going short. Like the split portfolio, it works particularly well for investors who have assets divided between taxable accounts and nontaxable retirement accounts.

Don is a 59-year-old widower with three grown children and a net worth of more than $4 million. He makes a good living as a physician, and he has plenty of money left to invest each month after covering his expenses. He holds $500,000 of his assets in a SEP-IRA as he owns his own medical practice, $100,000 of his assets in an IRA, and the remaining $3.5 million in taxable accounts. He wants to keep his taxable investing fairly conservative because he is considering early retirement and does not wish to generate taxes that come with trading in a taxable account. In his SEP-IRA, however, he wishes to trade his holdings and be able to go up to 100 percent long and 100 percent short depending on liquidity conditions.

Some of his taxable money is invested in Treasury Inflation Protected Securities (TIPS), which he holds in a TreasuryDirect account with the U.S. Treasury. The remainder is invested in Vanguard mutual funds: 60 percent in the Vanguard Total Stock Market Index Fund (VTSMX) and 40 percent in the Vanguard Limited-Term Tax-Exempt Fund (VMLTX). He does not wish to incur taxes trading in a taxable account, so he follows a dollar-cost averaging strategy. He contributes $1,000 per month to his Vanguard taxable accounts, which he allocates according to current liquidity conditions. (See Table 10.7.) He rebalances his accounts once every two years to maintain roughly the same allocation of 60 percent stocks and 40 percent bonds.

Don holds his nontaxable assets in a SEP-IRA and an IRA. The SEP-IRA currently holds $500,000 in assets, and the IRA holds $100,000 in assets. He is able to invest $36,000 per year into his SEP-IRA and $4,000 per

TABLE 10.7 Long-Short Split Portfolio: Taxable Contributions

Liquidity	VTSMX	VMLTX
Strongly bullish	$1,000 (100%)	$0 (0%)
Bullish	$750 (75%)	$250 (25%)
Neutral	$500 (50%)	$500 (50%)
Bearish	$250 (25%)	$750 (75%)
Strongly bearish	$0 (0%)	$1,000 (100%)

year in his IRA. He wishes to use timing, trading, and short selling in his retirement portfolio, but he does not feel comfortable using leverage. To execute this strategy, Don uses one no-load mutual fund and two ETFs in both his SEP-IRA and his IRA. He holds both IRAs at a discount brokerage. The no-load mutual fund is the Rydex Ursa Fund (RYURX), which is 100 percent short the S&P 500. In other words, when the S&P 500 declines 5 percent, the Rydex Ursa Fund rises 5 percent, and vice versa. The two ETFs are the iShares S&P 500 Index (IVV) and the iShares Lehman 1-3 Year Treasury Bond Fund (SHY).

Each month, Don contributes $3,000 to his SEP-IRA and $330 to his IRA, adding $40 to his $330 contribution in December to bring his annual IRA contribution to $4,000, which he allocates according to liquidity conditions. For example, Table 10.8 shows how he allocates his monthly SEP-IRA contribution according to current liquidity conditions. Note that when liquidity is strongly bullish, he is 100 percent long, and when liquidity is strongly bearish, he is 100 percent short. When liquidity is neutral, he is 100 percent invested in short-term bonds. He could adjust these allocations depending on his risk tolerance.

Don does not merely allocate his monthly contributions. He trades his SEP-IRA and his IRA holdings each fortnight according to current liquidity conditions. Table 10.9 shows how he would invest his SEP-IRA holdings. If liquidity were bearish at the beginning of one month, he would hold $300,000 (60 percent) in RYURX and $200,000 (40 percent) in SHY. If liquidity turned neutral the next week, he would sell all of his $300,000 holdings in RYURX and invest all of it into SHY, which would place all of his SEP-IRA into short-term bonds.

This strategy may seem aggressive. After all, Don is actively trading $600,000 in assets, and he goes 100 percent short as well as 100 percent long with these assets. Remember, though, Don has a net worth of more than $4 million, and he is actively trading only 15 percent of his net worth.

TABLE 10.8 Long-Short Split Portfolio: Nontaxable Contributions

Liquidity	RYURX	SHY	IVV
Strongly bullish	$0 (0%)	$0 (0%)	$3,000 (100%)
Bullish	$0 (0%)	$1,200 (40%)	$1,800 (60%)
Neutral	$0 (0%)	$3,000 (100%)	$0 (0%)
Bearish	$1,800 (60%)	$1,200 (40%)	$0 (0%)
Strongly bearish	$3,000 (100%)	$0 (0%)	$0 (0%)

TABLE 10.9 Long-Short Split Portfolio: Nontaxable Holdings

Liquidity	RYURX	SHY	IVV
Strongly bullish	$0 (0%)	$0 (0%)	$500,000 (100%)
Bullish	$0 (0%)	$200,000 (40%)	$300,000 (60%)
Neutral	$0 (0%)	$500,000 (100%)	$0 (0%)
Bearish	$300,000 (60%)	$200,000 (40%)	$0 (0%)
Strongly bearish	$500,000 (100%)	$0 (0%)	$0 (0%)

CONCLUSION

If you are looking for a lower-risk strategy to put the power of liquidity theory to work in your portfolio, hopefully these four strategies have given you some useful ideas. Nearly an infinite number of lower-risk strategies are possible using liquidity theory, and the four strategies discussed in this chapter are merely examples. You can easily adjust the allocations, investment vehicles, and investment strategies to suit your own needs. No matter what strategy you choose, be sure it suits your time horizon and your risk tolerance before you implement it.

CHAPTER 11

Swinging for the Fences: More Aggressive Strategies

This chapter focuses on higher-risk liquidity strategies, which are designed primarily for two groups of investors:

1. High-net-worth individuals, whom we define an individuals with more than $5 million in investable assets.
2. Institutional investors, such as hedge funds and pension funds.

For investors with substantial assets, these strategies put the full power of liquidity theory to work. The risks of these strategies, however, make them inappropriate for most individual investors. If you are an individual investor with less than $5 million in investable assets and you choose to use one of these strategies, we would recommend limiting it to a very small portion of your portfolio.

LEVERAGE

What distinguishes most of the strategies in this chapter from those in the previous chapter is the use of leverage, or borrowed money. An investor using leverage borrows money at a fixed interest rate and invests the borrowed money along with his or her own money. The investor must repay the borrowed amount to the lender with interest. Obviously the investor hopes the investment return using the borrowed money is higher than the interest cost of the borrowed money.

Suppose a high-net-worth individual allocates $2 million to short the S&P 500. To short the S&P 500 by 200 percent of the value of her allocation, she borrows $2 million from a brokerage firm at 4 percent interest and invests the borrowed $2 million along with her $2 million allocation.

Suppose she follows this strategy for one year. At the end of the year, she returns $2.08 million to the brokerage firm, which includes the $2 million she borrowed along with $80,000 in interest ($2 million × 4 percent = $80,000). She hopes her profit on this trade exceeds the value of the $80,000 interest payment to the brokerage firm. Suppose the S&P falls 10 percent during the year. Since she is 200 percent short the S&P 500, her portfolio gains 20 percent, or $400,000. She owes the brokerage firm $80,000 in interest on the $2 million she borrowed, so her profit on this trade is $320,000 ($400,000 − $80,000 = $320,000), or 16 percent. Suppose, however, the S&P 500 rises 10 percent during the year. Since she is 200 percent short the S&P 500, her portfolio loses 20 percent, or $400,000. She owes the brokerage firm $80,000 in interest, so her loss on this trade is $480,000 (−$400,000 − $80,000 = −$480,000), or 24 percent.

Obviously leverage multiplies the downside as well as the upside. If an investor is leveraged 200 percent to the S&P 500 by borrowing 50 percent of the money he invests, his portfolio will rise and fall 2 percent for every 1 percent rise and fall in the S&P 500. While a 50 percent gain in the S&P 500 would double his money, a 50 percent decline in the S&P 500 would wipe out his investment (and he would also owe the interest on the borrowed amount). For example, if an investor had the misfortune of going 200 percent long the S&P 500 from March 2000 until October 2002, he would have lost all of his invested money. The use of leverage dramatically increases risk in a portfolio. We would advise individual investors with less than $5 million in assets to avoid the use of leverage.

Due to the trading and leverage involved, the strategies in this chapter are best implemented with exchange-traded funds (ETFs) or stock index futures. Unlike the vast majority of mutual funds, these vehicles allow investors to go short as well as long.

Long-Short Trading

Timed contributions: No

Trading: Yes

Short positions: Yes

Leverage: No

This strategy is the most conservative in this chapter because it does not use leverage. It is suitable for high-net-worth investors who wish to trade a chunk of their assets aggressively on a regular basis but do not wish to use leverage.

Carl and Jane recently sold their restaurant supply business for $8 million in cash after taxes. Both of them are in their mid-50s with two children still in college. The couple allocates $3 million to a portfolio of laddered municipal bonds to preserve capital. They also invest $2 million in a leading fund of hedge funds. With the remaining $3 million, they decide to create their own "liquidity hedge fund." Since they have a substantial cushion of more conservative assets, they wish to trade this $3 million aggressively on a weekly basis. Carl was burned badly by a leveraged investment many years ago, so he intends to keep the promise he made to himself that he would never use leverage again.

With $3 million from the sale of their business, Carl and Jane open an account with a brokerage firm. Initially, they place all $3 million into a money market fund. To execute their strategy, they use three Barclays Global Investors ETFs: iShares S&P 500 Index (IVV), iShares Russell 2000 Index (IWM), and iShares Lehman 1-3 Year Treasury Bond Fund (SHY). Table 11.1 shows how they allocate their $3 million according to current liquidity conditions.

When liquidity is strongly bullish, Carl and Jane use 50 percent of their portfolio's value ($1.5 million) to go 100 percent long IWM and 50 percent of their portfolio's value ($1.5 million) to go 100 percent long IVV. By contrast, when liquidity is strongly bearish, they use 50 percent of their portfolio's value ($1.5 million) to go 100 percent short IWM and 50 percent of their portfolio's value ($1.5 million) to go 100 percent short IVV. When liquidity is neutral, they hold 100 percent of their portfolio ($3 million) in SHY. The use of IWM should enhance their returns. The Russell 2000 is composed of small-capitalization stocks, many of which are more speculative. These stocks tend to perform better than the overall market during periods of strongly bullish liquidity and worse than the overall market during periods of strongly bearish liquidity.

Here is a short example of how Carl and Jane would trade their "liquidity hedge fund." Suppose liquidity were bearish during the first week they began using this strategy in their $3,000,000 portfolio. They would

TABLE 11.1 Long-Short Trading

Liquidity	IWM	IVV	SHY
Strongly bullish	50% (100% long)	50% (100% long)	0%
Bullish	25% (100% long)	75% (100% long)	0%
Neutral	0%	0%	100% (100% long)
Bearish	25% (100% short)	75% (100% short)	0%
Strongly bearish	50% (100% short)	50% (100% short)	0%

hold 25 percent of their portfolio ($750,000) in a 100 percent short position in IWM and 75 percent of their portfolio ($2,250,000) in a 100 percent short position in IVV. At the end of the week, suppose their strategy was successful, and their portfolio increased in value to $3,040,000 ($765,000 in IWM and $2,275,000 in IVV). If liquidity turned strongly bearish the next week, they would liquidate $755,000 of their 100 percent short position in IVV and use the proceeds to go 100 percent short in IWM. Thus, they would have $1,520,000 invested 100 percent short in IWM and $1,520,000 invested 100 percent short in IVV. Suppose this strategy was not as successful. After three weeks of strongly bearish liquidity, their account declined to $3,020,000 ($1,505,000 in IWM and $1,515,000 in IVV). Suppose liquidity suddenly turned neutral as major cash takeovers were announced and new offerings slowed during a holiday. Carl and Jane would sell all of their open positions in IVV and IWM and invest all of their $3,020,000 portfolio in SHY. Suppose their portfolio rose to $3,025,000 after two weeks in neutral. Then liquidity turned bullish. They would invest 25 percent of their portfolio ($756,250) in a 100 percent long position in IWM and 75 percent of their portfolio ($2,268,750) in a 100 percent long position in IVV.

This strategy not only involves considerable risks, but it also incurs brokerage costs, and every trade has tax consequences. Carl and Jane are comfortable with the risks of this strategy because they own considerable assets, and they invested over a third of the proceeds of the sale of their business in conservative municipal bonds. They are willing to follow this strategy because they are convinced the benefits of liquidity theory over time will outweigh the trading costs and taxes they will incur using this strategy. Also, as high-net-worth individuals, they are eligible for substantial discounts on trading commissions from their brokerage firm, and they can afford to hire an accountant to handle investment recordkeeping and income tax preparation for them. Once again, however, we caution that an aggressive active trading strategy like this one is not suitable for most individual investors.

Leveraged Long-Short Trading

Timed contributions: No

Trading: Yes

Short positions: Yes

Leverage: Yes

The next strategy is the first one that uses leverage. It is a variation on the long-short active trading strategy just described. It is suitable for high-net-worth investors and institutional investors who wish to use leverage while trading their assets aggressively on a regular basis.

Suppose Carl overcomes his aversion to leverage and the couple decides to use it in their $3 million "liquidity hedge fund." They use two of the ETFs mentioned in the strategy described earlier: iShares S&P 500 Index (IVV) and iShares Lehman 1-3 Year Treasury Bond Fund (SHY). They also use a margin account at their brokerage firm to go up to 200 percent long and 200 percent short in IVV. For example, if their strategy called for 100 percent of their portfolio to be 200 percent long the S&P 500, they would invest their $3 million portfolio in IVV and borrow an additional $3 million from their brokerage firm to invest in IVV. Table 11.2 shows how they allocate their portfolio each week according to current liquidity conditions.

Note that this example introduces cautiously bullish and cautiously bearish options, which give Carl and Jane more flexibility in their portfolio. They adopt a liquidity position according to the daily estimated net change in the trading float of shares (L1) as shown in Table 11.3. The couple's margin account allows them to go both 200 percent long and 200 percent short in IVV with up to 100 percent of their portfolio. At the same time, they hold positions in short-term bonds during periods when liquidity is not particularly bullish or bearish.

Suppose a hedge fund wishes to implement this strategy. One of the most convenient ways to execute it would be to use a combination of S&P 500 futures and three-month Treasury bills. S&P 500 futures are traded on the Chicago Mercantile Exchange (CME) in terms of contracts. Each S&P 500 futures contract buys or sells a fixed value of the S&P 500. The value of the futures contract is defined as the value of the S&P 500 multiplied by $250, an amount the CME sets in the contract specifications:

$$1 \text{ S\&P 500 Futures Contract} = \$250 \times \text{Value of S\&P 500}$$

TABLE 11.2 Leveraged Long-Short Trading: ETFs

Liquidity	IVV	SHY
Strongly bullish	100% (200% long)	0%
Bullish	100% (100% long)	0%
Cautiously bullish	50% (100% long)	50% (100% long)
Neutral	0%	100% (100% long)
Cautiously bearish	50% (100% short)	50% (100% long)
Bearish	100% (100% short)	0%
Strongly bearish	100% (200% short)	0%

TABLE 11.3   Liquidity Stances

Daily L1	Stance
<–$800 million	Strongly bullish
–$500 million to –$800 million	Bullish
–$200 million to –$500 million	Cautiously bullish
–$200 million to $200 million	Neutral
$200 million to $500 million	Cautiously bearish
$500 million to $800 million	Bearish
>$800 million	Strongly bearish

If the S&P 500 stands at 1,000, then each S&P 500 futures contract is worth $250,000 ($250 per contract × 1,000). Thus, if a hedge fund wanted to invest $100 million in the S&P 500 using S&P 500 futures when the value of the S&P 500 stood at 1,000, it would buy 400 S&P 500 futures contracts ($250,000 per contract × 400 contracts = $100 million). S&P 500 futures contracts are settled on a cash basis—no one actually takes delivery of the stocks in the index—on a specified settlement date. The profit or loss on a futures contract is the difference between the value of the contract on the purchase date and the value of the contract on the settlement date.

To go up to 200 percent long or 200 percent short the S&P 500, a hedge fund would buy or sell S&P 500 futures contracts equal to 200 percent of the underlying value of its portfolio. Using this strategy, Table 11.4 shows how the hedge fund allocates its portfolio according to current liquidity conditions.

This strategy uses just two investment vehicles, so it is quite simple to execute. The next two strategies use multiple stock index futures for additional flexibility.

TABLE 11.4   Leveraged Long-Short Trading: Futures

Liquidity	S&P 500 Futures	Three-Month Treasury Bills
Strongly bullish	100% (200% long)	0%
Bullish	100% (100% long)	0%
Cautiously bullish	50% (100% long)	50%
Neutral	0%	100%
Cautiously bearish	50% (100% short)	50%
Bearish	100% (100% short)	0%
Strongly bearish	100% (200% short)	0%

Futures Trading

Timed contributions: No

Trading: Yes

Short positions: Yes

Leverage: Yes

This strategy is similar to the one used in the TrimTabs model futures portfolio, which currently exists only on paper. It is most suitable for institutional investors, particularly hedge funds. It uses futures contracts for multiple indexes, providing maximum flexibility for traders who wish to tailor their portfolios as specifically as possible to current market conditions.

A $2 billion hedge fund decides to devote 20 percent of its assets, or $400 million, to a liquidity-based strategy. It desires complete trading flexibility, including the use of short positions and leverage of up to 200 percent of its portfolio's underlying value. To execute this strategy, it uses four investment vehicles: S&P 500 futures, Nasdaq-100 futures, Russell 2000 futures, and three-month Treasury bills. The use of multiple indexes allows the hedge fund to adapt its portfolio more closely to market conditions than the previous strategy. Like S&P 500 futures, Russell 2000 and Nasdaq-100 futures are traded on the Chicago Mercantile Exchange in terms of contracts:

1 Nasdaq-100 Futures Contract = $100 × Value of Nasdaq-100

1 Russell 2000 Futures Contract = $500 × Value of Russell 2000

If a hedge fund wanted to assume a $500 million short position in the Nasdaq-100 and the value of the Nasdaq-100 were 1,500, it would sell 3,333 Nasdaq-100 futures contracts ($500 million ÷ $150,000 per contract = 3,333 contracts). Similarly, if a hedge fund wanted to assume a $200 million long position in the Russell 2000 and the value of the Russell 2000 were 500, it would buy 800 Russell 2000 futures contracts ($200 million ÷ $250,000 per contract = 800 contracts). Table 11.5 shows how the hedge fund allocates its portfolio according to current liquidity conditions.

When liquidity is strongly bullish or strongly bearish, the hedge fund goes long and short futures that track the Nasdaq-100 and Russell 2000, which are more volatile than S&P 500 futures. When liquidity is bullish or bearish, the hedge fund has the freedom to use either a combination of

TABLE 11.5   Futures Trading

Liquidity	Portfolio
Strongly bullish	50% (200% long) Nasdaq-100, 50% (200% long) Russell 2000
Bullish	50% (100% long) Nasdaq-100, 50% (100% long) Russell 2000
	or
	100% (100% long) S&P 500
Cautiously bullish	50% (100% long) S&P 500, 50% 3-month Treasury bills
Neutral	100% 3-month Treasury bills
Cautiously bearish	50% (100% short) S&P 500, 50% 3-month Treasury bills
Bearish	50% (100% short) Nasdaq-100, 50% (100% short) Russell 2000
	or
	100% (100% short) S&P 500
Strongly bearish	50% (200% short) Nasdaq-100, 50% (200% short) Russell 2000

Nasdaq-100 and Russell 2000 futures (when the market is tilted toward the speculative side) or S&P 500 futures (when the market appears less speculative). Of course, the combinations in Table 11.5 could be altered if market conditions warranted. For example, if the hedge fund believed the overall liquidity environment were cautiously bullish even as technology shares were subject to rampant speculation, it could go 50 percent long S&P 500 futures and go 50 percent short Nasdaq-100 futures.

Aggressive Futures Trading

Timed contributions: No

Trading: Yes

Short positions: Yes

Leverage: Yes

This strategy is most suitable for hedge funds. It is identical to the long-short futures trading strategy, except it uses combinations of long and short positions when liquidity is cautiously bullish or cautiously bearish and permits the use of leverage of up to 400 percent of the portfolio's underlying value.

Suppose the $2 billion hedge fund mentioned previously wished to use this more aggressive strategy. Table 11.6 shows how it allocates its portfolio according to current liquidity conditions.

Note that this strategy offers the hedge fund considerable flexibility to adapt its portfolio to market conditions. For example, when liquidity is cautiously bullish, it can choose to keep 50 percent of its portfolio in three-month Treasury bills and 50 percent of its portfolio 100 percent long the S&P 500, or it can choose to keep 66 percent of its portfolio 100 percent long the S&P 500 and 33 percent of its portfolio 100 percent short the Nasdaq-100. The latter option would be particularly useful if overall liquidity was cautiously bullish but the hedge fund believed the technology sector was still frothy. Also, this strategy is 400 percent leveraged during strongly bullish and strongly bearish periods. Thus, if the hedge fund allocates $400 million to this liquidity strategy, it could command a maximum of $1.6 billion, which is four times the value of its underlying portfolio.

TABLE 11.6 Aggressive Futures Trading

Liquidity	Portfolio
Strongly bullish	50% (400% long) Nasdaq-100, 50% (400% long) Russell 2000
Bullish	50% (200% long) Nasdaq-100, 50% (200% long) Russell 2000 or 100% (200% long) S&P 500
Cautiously bullish	50% (100% long) S&P 500, 50% 3-month Treasury bills or 67% (100% long) S&P 500, 33% (100% short) Nasdaq-100
Neutral	100% 3-month Treasury bills
Cautiously bearish	50% (100% short) S&P 500, 50% 3-month Treasury bills or 67% (100% short) Nasdaq-100, 33% (100% long) S&P 500
Bearish	50% (200% short) Nasdaq-100, 50% (200% short) Russell 2000 or 100% (200% short) S&P 500
Strongly bearish	50% (400% short) Nasdaq-100, 50% (400% short) Russell 2000

CONCLUSION

The more aggressive strategies in this chapter should outperform the more conservative strategies in the previous chapter, but they also involve much more risk. If you are not a high-net-worth individual or an institutional investor, we urge you to think very carefully before using these higher-risk strategies. Unless you are an experienced investor with significant assets who is committed to tracking liquidity on at least a weekly basis, you would likely be better served by the lower-risk strategies outlined in Chapter 10.

Looking Ahead

Managing Difficulties

Throughout this book, we have extolled the virtues of liquidity theory in predicting the direction of the stock market. No system is perfect, however, and we will be the first to concede that liquidity theory is not an exception. In this chapter, we discuss some of the difficulties facing followers of liquidity theory and how they can manage them.

INCOMPLETE AND DELAYED INFORMATION

Perhaps the most significant challenge for liquidity theory is incomplete and delayed information. Often we must settle for estimated data rather than actual data, or we must wait several weeks for data that is already outdated once it is released. Our market forecast depends to a great extent on reliable corporate finance and funds flow data. Nevertheless, after tracking stock market liquidity for 15 years, we have devised ways to account for the deficiencies of the data. That is why liquidity theory remains an art as well as a science.

The components of our formula that estimates the net change in the trading float of shares (L1) present a number of interpretive challenges. While the number and dollar amounts of new stock buybacks and new cash takeovers are relatively straightforward to determine, the exact timing of their impact on the stock market is a different matter. We count new stock buybacks in our liquidity formula on the day they are announced. In reality, however, buybacks do not occur on the exact date they are announced. Public companies usually repurchase their own shares over a period of anywhere from 12 to 24 months. This time lag presents problems for liquidity theory. For example, suppose Wal-Mart announces a two-year, $5 billion share repurchase program. While this buyback registers in our liquidity formula on the day it is announced, its impact on the market is felt over a two-year period. If a few large buybacks are announced in a single week, they can provide a distorted view of actual liquidity because their impact will not be felt until months or even years after they are announced. We manage this difficulty in two ways. First, we track the number as well as the dollar amount of buybacks announced each week. The weekly number of buybacks is usually a more reliable barometer of the attitudes of corporate America than the weekly dollar amount. We would expect to see a large number of deals—not just a few large deals—when corporate America is bullish. Second, we estimate actual stock buybacks using the relationship between the number and dollar amount of new stock buybacks over the previous four weeks and the historic averages of the number and dollar amount of new stock buybacks.

Another issue that potentially affects buyback data is whether public companies actually buy back all of the shares they announce they will. Each year, we examine the amount of actual buybacks of the 100 stocks with the largest market capitalizations. We have found these megacap companies do actually buy back all of the announced authorizations over periods ranging from 12 to 24 months. Of course, this sample is quite small, and smaller, less financially secure firms do not always complete their announced buybacks. Thus, we guess that at least 90 percent of announced buybacks are actually completed.

Cash takeovers present the same difficulty as stock buybacks. While their number and dollar amounts are widely reported in the media, it is impossible to track exactly when a takeover impacts stock market liquidity. When a cash takeover is announced, arbitrageurs typically buy the shares of the target company, removing them from the trading float of shares. Depending on the terms of the takeover and market conditions, however, the timing of their intervention is impossible to determine with precision. Since arbitrageurs typically snap up two-thirds of the trading float of the target company within a week of a deal's announcement, we count two-thirds of the value of a cash takeover in our liquidity formula when it is announced.

On the other side of the corporate liquidity ledger, new offerings do not present the same timing difficulties as stock buybacks and cash takeovers. Initial public offerings, secondary offerings, and convertibles are widely reported in the media and are typically priced shortly before they are sold. We add 15 percent to the dollar amount of a new offering to account for the "green shoe"—the option of the underwriter to purchase additional shares equal to 15 percent of the total number of shares floated. Insider selling, however, presents two challenges. First, not all insiders must report their selling to the U.S. Securities and Exchange Commission on Form 4 and Form 144. To account for selling by smaller insiders, we double reported insider selling to estimate total insider selling. Second, reports of insider selling reach the public several weeks in arrears. As we discuss in Chapter 14, requiring weekly reporting of major insider sales would be one of the most useful tools that regulators could provide for stock market investors.

We use U.S. equity fund flows (L2) as a proxy for individual investment in the stock market, which presents several difficulties. First, while the Investment Company Institute (ICI) reports U.S. equity fund, global equity fund, and bond and hybrid fund flow data on a monthly basis, it is released on a delay of several weeks. To track fund flows on a daily and weekly basis, TrimTabs produces its own estimates. There is currently no way for us to track flows at every one of the thousands of funds available—there are about 4,700 equity funds alone. So we track flows at about 80 fund families on a daily basis. These fund families have assets equal to 15 percent of all ICI equity fund assets and 13 percent of all ICI bond fund assets. We regress these numbers by sector to estimate daily flows for the various fund categories. While regression analysis is a useful technique, it cannot estimate fund flows with complete accuracy. Thus, we revise our monthly flow estimates using data provided by Fidelity, Janus, MFSS, and Vanguard, four of the largest fund families not included in the 15 percent of all U.S. equity funds we track daily. Sometimes the revisions are significant. For example, in late 2003 after the stale-price trading scandals involving Janus, Putnam, and other well-known mutual funds families, Vanguard and Fidelity began receiving proportionally more inflows as investors sought fund families untainted by the scandals. Thus, our monthly total of U.S. equity fund flows (L2) changes three times:

1. Our first monthly estimate is based on TrimTabs' daily fund flow estimates.
2. Our second monthly estimate revises our first monthly estimate based on fund flow data from Fidelity, Janus, MFSS, and Vanguard, as well as Schwab's customers' fund purchases.
3. The ICI releases actual monthly data several weeks in arrears.

Second, U.S. equity funds are not the only way for individuals to invest in equities. Individuals may also buy individual stocks directly and invest in exchange-traded funds (ETFs). Unfortunately, however, there is currently no way to measure how much money individuals invest directly in individual stocks. And while *TrimTabs Exchange-Traded Funds* tracks flows of all ETFs on a daily basis, we have no way to know the source of the flows. In short, we must settle for U.S. equity fund flows even though we know they provide an incomplete picture of individual flows into and out of the U.S. stock market. To estimate the total amount of money flowing into equities—including mutual funds, ETFs, and direct investments—we double U.S. equity fund flows. Since investors pumped $127 billion into U.S. equity funds in 2003, we estimate that $254 billion flowed into U.S. equities in that year.

Margin debt data (L3) reaches the public on a significant delay. The New York Stock Exchange reports margin debt growth at its member firms, but data for one month does not arrive until late in the following month. Once the public receives this data, it is already outdated. More timely reporting of margin debt growth would benefit investors.

INVESTOR PSYCHOLOGY

Investor psychology also presents challenges for liquidity analysis because investors do not always behave rationally. An entire subfield of economics—behavioral finance—has devoted itself to understanding investor behavior. This research has demonstrated that investors are by no means rational actors. Often they make impulsive decisions based on emotions rather than logic, allowing fear and greed to drive their investing decisions. For example, even if L1—the best leading indicator of stock market performance—turns strongly bullish after a brutal bear market, investors may continue to pull money from the stock market. Conversely, even if L1 turns strongly bearish during a bubble, investors may continue dumping money into the stock market because of hefty gains they have enjoyed in the recent past.

How does liquidity theory cope with shifting investor attitudes? Many professional investors rely on surveys, such as the American Association of Individual Investors Investor Sentiment Survey and the Investors Intelligence Survey, to gauge investor sentiment. While we do review these surveys, we do not conduct any sentiment surveys ourselves because we are far more interested in what investors do rather than how they say they feel. We also believe the behavior of investors who act irrationally tends to be highly predictable. In fact, if investors are behaving extremely irrationally, a market top or a market bottom is probably imminent. To measure investor sentiment, we use two of the trim tabs of liquidity theory: U.S. equity fund flows (L2) and margin debt (L3). If L2 and L3 are surging as L1 is strongly bearish, a market top is probably imminent. Conversely, if L2 and L3 are plunging as L1 is strongly bullish, a market bottom is probably near. Timing market tops and market bottoms is never easy, but using L2 and L3 to gauge investor psychology can be extremely helpful.

EXOGENOUS SHOCKS

Followers of liquidity theory face the same investment risks posed by exogenous shocks—including terrorism, political unrest, and acts of nature—as all other investors do. By itself, liquidity theory cannot predict these events. What liquidity theory can do, however, is help investors take advantage of the opportunities these exogenous shocks offer.

Often exogenous factors cause dramatic, if short-lived, shifts in stock market liquidity. Perhaps the best recent example of an exogenous shock is the September 11, 2001, terrorist attacks. After terrorists hijacked four commercial airliners and crashed three of them into the World Trade Center and the Pentagon, the U.S. stock market shut down for four days. Business activity ground to a halt, and many Americans were glued to television coverage of the attacks. Once the U.S. stock market reopened on September 17, 2001, the S&P 500 plunged 12 percent over the next five days. Figure 12.1, which plots estimated daily flows for U.S. equity funds in September 2001, reveals the scale of the panic.

During September 2001, investors sold $27.3 billion in U.S. equity funds, the second-largest one-month outflow in history. Clearly the players were folding en masse in the stock market casino. Yet who was on the other side of these trades? As usual, it was the house. Figure 12.2 plots daily stock buybacks in September 2001.

In September 2001, public companies announced $53.6 billion worth of buybacks of their own shares, an all-time record high. Investors who followed liquidity theory cut through the hype of the talking heads on the

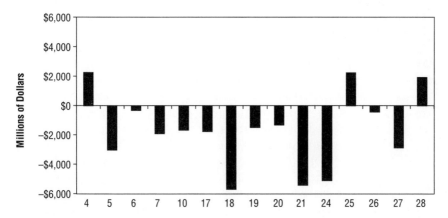

FIGURE 12.1 Estimated Daily Flows for U.S. Equity Funds, September 2001
Source: TrimTabs Investment Research.

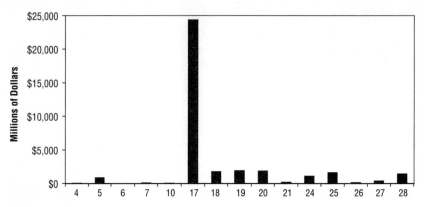

FIGURE 12.2   Daily New Stock Buybacks, September 2001
Source: TrimTabs Investment Research.

cable networks and huckster analysts. They would have realized that while the dumb money in the stock market casino—the players—was selling a near-record amount of shares in U.S. equity funds, the smartest money in the casino—public companies—was buying their own shares with both hands. Can liquidity theory predict exogenous shocks such as terrorist attacks in advance? Of course not. Can liquidity theory help investors take advantage of the short-term investing opportunities exogenous shocks can present? Absolutely. Investors who bought stocks shortly after the September 11 attacks have since been handsomely rewarded in the equity markets.

MANAGING WHAT WE DO NOT KNOW WE DO NOT KNOW

One of the greatest pitfalls facing investors, including followers of liquidity theory, is the information they do not know they do not know. What does this mean for liquidity theory? Occasionally information exists that, if we knew we did not know it, would radically alter our interpretation of current liquidity data and thus our forecast of the stock market's performance. One of the best recent examples of this difficulty came shortly before hostilities began in Iraq in 2003. On March 13, 2003, two days after the market bottomed, Charles Biderman predicted on Bloomberg Television that the overall stock market would pop 20 percent to 25 percent once investors realized the Iraq war would not be fought in the United States. By the end of April 2003, the TrimTabs model futures portfolio had gained 9 percent. When L1 turned bearish in May 2003, so did our model portfolio.

At this point, information we did not know we did not know began to affect our model portfolio's performance. We failed to anticipate that hedge funds that had entered the second quarter of 2003 either net short or drastically underinvested would pump at least $200 billion into equities during the second quarter of 2003. We also failed to anticipate that pension fund sponsors, including municipalities, not only dumped huge amounts of cash into their pension plans but also sold massive amounts of long-term bonds during the second quarter. These sponsors invested the net proceeds of these bond sales into their pension funds, which used at least half of the net proceeds to buy stocks. Inflows from hedge funds and pension funds—much of which are not reflected in L2 because these players invest substantial proportions of their cash through direct investment in stocks or through ETFs—provided a large share of the fuel that drove the stock market steadily higher in the spring of 2003.

As insider selling rose to record bearish levels by the early summer of 2003, we waited for the new offering calendar to spike and absorb all of the cash flooding into the market. We expected new offerings would top $30 billion monthly, as they did during February 2000 to March 2000. While new offerings did rise to their highest level since early 2002, the calendar reached only $24.9 billion in May 2003, $25.8 billion in June 2003, and $24.5 billion in July 2003. We continued waiting for the calendar to spike in August 2003 and September 2003, but it never did. In fact, new offerings actually fell to $9.9 billion in August and $19.8 billion in September. We discovered the reason for the lack of new offerings a few months too late: firings at Wall Street corporate finance departments during 2002 limited the ability of companies to generate new offerings. Once we realized the shrinking ranks of the "white shoe" crowd would limit the ability of public companies to sell shares, we finally turned bullish at the end of October 2003 and made back some of our earlier losses.

As this example shows, sometimes what one does not know can be as important as what one does know. We are always watchful for what we do not know about liquidity and the stock market. Humility and constant openness to new ideas are essential ingredients for successful stock market investing.

A WORK IN PROGRESS: PART ART AND PART SCIENCE

TrimTabs began developing liquidity theory 15 years ago, but it remains a work in progress. Over time, we have changed how we calculate and interpret our liquidity indicators. For example, until September 2000, we combined corporate liquidity (L1) and U.S. equity funds inflows (L2). After observing a sharp divergence between the actions of corporate investors and individual investors in 1999 and 2000, we decided it made sense to separate corporate flows from fund flows in our liquidity formula. After all, corporate flows are a better leading indicator of stock market direction, and fund flows are a lagging, contrary indicator.

More recently, we made two changes in our tracking of stock buybacks. First, we began including the number of buybacks along with the dollar amount in our daily liquidity updates. Often a small number of massive large-capitalization buybacks masks an overall low level of corporate buying. For example, during the week ended Thursday, April 1, 2004, $13.1 billion in buybacks was announced. While this large dollar amount might appear to signal corporate bullishness, only nine buybacks were announced that week, and three of them—a $7 billion buyback for PepsiCo, a $5 billion buyback for ChevronTexaco, and a $1 billion buyback for Clear Channel Communications—accounted for nearly all of the weekly dollar amount. The number of buybacks often is a more reliable indicator of whether public companies see more value in cash or in their own shares.

Second, we introduced an alternative way to calculate stock buyback activity. In addition to calculating buybacks based on new stock buyback announcements, we also estimate actual buybacks based on the daily average number and dollar amount of new stock buybacks over the past two years modified by the number and dollar amount of new stock buyback announcements. How does estimating actual buybacks instead of using newly announced buybacks affect our view of liquidity? Let's return to the example of the week ended Thursday, April 1, 2004. On the one hand, using new stock buyback announcements sets the dollar amount of buybacks at $2.6 billion daily ($13.1 billion weekly ÷ 5 days in the week = $2.6 billion daily). This dollar amount is extremely bullish. On the other hand, estimating actual buybacks suggests far less buyback activity was actually occurring. New stock buybacks averaged $3.5 billion weekly ($700 million daily) over the two years before the week ended June 1, 2004, and we estimate that they ranged from about $300 million to $900 million daily. During the week ended April 1, 2004, nine buybacks were announced, which would place actual buybacks at the lower end of the two-year range of $300 million to $900 million daily. Thus, estimating actual buybacks would place buyback activity at only about $500 million daily rather than $2.6 billion daily.

Which buyback figure is more accurate? Each method of calculating buybacks has its advantages. While new stock buybacks provide a more real-time picture of corporate sentiment, shares are actually repurchased over periods of months and years. While estimating actual buybacks smooths weekly fluctuations, estimates are based on past data rather than present activity. Still, the actual level of buybacks is probably closer to the figured derived by estimating actual buybacks than the one derived by using new stock buybacks, since actual buyback activity on any given day is the result of buybacks announced months or years earlier. In the example, actual buyback activity was likely much closer to $500 million daily than $2.6 billion daily.

Finally, we have begun to estimate the amount of cash moving into and out of the stock market on a daily basis to help us predict the direction of the stock market with more precision. As explained in Chapter 6, we use a modified version of our liquidity formula to estimate corporate liquidity (L1) during the coming week:

Estimated Daily L1 = New Offerings + Insider Selling
$\qquad$ – Actual Stock Buybacks – $\frac{2}{3}$ New Cash Takeovers

We use expected new offerings and recent data on insider selling, actual stock buybacks, and new cash takeovers in this formula. Here is how it might appear for a particular week:

$\qquad$ Estimated L1 = $1 Billion Daily + $500 Million Daily
$\qquad\qquad$ – $600 Million Daily – $350 Million Daily
$\qquad\qquad$ = $550 Million Daily

During this particular week, we estimate that corporate liquidity would be bearish by $550 million daily. Then we consider whether daily U.S. equity fund flows (L2) will likely turn overall liquidity more bullish or more bearish. For example, if we expected $800 million daily in U.S. equity fund inflows in this particular week, it would mean overall liquidity would be slightly bullish by $250 million daily ($550 million daily – $800 million daily = –$250 million daily). While our cash flow projections do not always prove correct, estimating the daily values of our liquidity components over the coming week helps us make better market calls.

Liquidity theory remains a work in progress. The basic concepts of liquidity theory are rooted in fundamental economic principles, but interpreting liquidity in the U.S. stock market is an art as well as a science. Liquidity analysis involves many interrelated factors, only a few of which can be quantified with any certainty in real time. We have no doubt that if we had accurate data for all of our liquidity trim tabs, we could consistently predict the performance of the stock market. Not all of the data is available, however, and some of what data is available is not released in real time. Sometimes you just have to make a call on a wing and a prayer and hope you are right.

CHAPTER 13

New Applications

Cash takeovers, stock buybacks, new offerings, insider selling, mutual funds flows, margin debt—the previous sections have shown how careful analysis of these factors can successfully predict the direction of the stock market. Nevertheless, our interest in liquidity is not limited to L1, L2, and L3. Numerous macroeconomic factors affect how much cash the house and the players have available for investment in the stock and bond markets. Two of the most important of these factors are income and employment. If incomes are rising and the labor market is robust, more money will be available for investment. Conversely, if incomes are falling and the labor market is tight, less money will be available for investment. We have developed innovative methods of measuring personal income, corporate income, employment growth, and labor market demand.

All of these indicators are measured by U.S. government statistics, but government statistics and sausage have one thing in common: One does not want to watch either being made. As we explain in this chapter, we believe our methods provide a more accurate picture of what is happening in the real economy. We also believe the corresponding U.S. government statistics should be treated with healthy degree of caution.

PERSONAL INCOME

To fully understand the amount of liquidity available for investment, we need to do more than track fund flows into and out of the equity and bond markets. We need to assess the health of the balance sheet of the United States as a whole, which depends to a significant extent on personal income. The stock markets, the bond markets, the U.S. economy— their health all depends on the aggregate personal income of everyone in the United States. While Wall Street analyzes the earnings of public companies to determine their value, we prefer to focus on personal income to determine how much cash will be available for investment in the equity and bond markets. We have found that personal income growth is highly correlated with the performance of the stock market. As incomes rise, more money is available for investment in the equity and bond markets, which bolsters equity markets. As incomes stagnate or fall, equity markets usually follow.

How can we track personal income? An obvious way would be to use the statistics in *Personal Income and Outlays*, a report released each month by the U.S. Bureau of Economic Analysis (BEA), an agency of the U.S. Department of Commerce. This report arrives a month in arrears; for example, January's data is released at the end of February or the beginning of March. Most Wall Street economists rely on the BEA's personal income data. The BEA's annual and semiannual estimates of personal income are fairly reliable, since the BEA compiles them from quarterly unemployment insurance reports collected from companies by each of the 50 states. The BEA's most recent monthly estimates of personal income, however, are notoriously unreliable. To calculate monthly personal income, the BEA "interpolates and extrapolates" semiannual data using monthly employment and population data from other government agencies. In other words, the BEA's personal income estimates for the most recent six months are nothing more than educated guesses based on data that is as much as six months old.

Unfortunately the BEA's monthly personal income estimates are most unreliable at times when sound estimates are most critical: when the economy is shifting from contraction to expansion or from expansion to contraction. For example, suppose the U.S. economy is making a transition from a business cycle bottom to a period of expansion. The BEA would almost certainly underestimate personal income over such a period because it would be calculating personal income based on data gathered during an earlier period of contraction. We have found that as the economy moves from contraction to expansion, the BEA underestimates growth in personal income by as much as 40 percent.

The best recent example of this problem occurred in 2003. From January 2003 to March 2003, investors were wracked by uncertainty over war in Iraq. Once major hostilities ended in April 2003, the U.S. economy began to recover. The BEA's personal income estimates, however, were exceedingly slow in reflecting the economic recovery. As late as September 2003, the BEA was calculating personal income based on data gathered before the outbreak of war in Iraq, when the economy was still contracting. Figure 13.1 shows that as late as March 2004, the BEA was still revising personal income from June 2003 through January 2004 dramatically up-

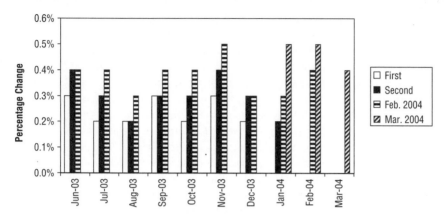

FIGURE 13.1   U.S. Bureau of Economic Analysis Monthly Revisions to Personal Income, June 2003 to March 2004
Source: U.S. Bureau of Economic Analysis.

ward. While the BEA eventually detected the acceleration in personal income that occurred in late 2003, it did so six months late.

We have developed a much better method of tracking personal income. Wages and salaries subject to withholding constitute roughly two-thirds of what the BEA terms personal income. We use the income and employment taxes withheld from wages and salaries to calculate personal income. Each day, the U.S. Treasury collects withheld income and employment tax data from approximately 130 million salaried U.S. workers, which it records in the Daily and Monthly Treasury Statements. Since withholdings are the correlate of wages and salaries—adjusting for changes in income tax rates—we are able to track changes in wages and salaries on a near real-time basis. As a proxy for personal income, this data provides a near real-time indication of whether personal income is rising or falling. Over the six years we have tracked this data, we have found that rising withheld income and employment tax collections—and thus rising personal incomes—are often an excellent leading indicator of the stock market's direction. Rising incomes mean additional cash is available for investment, while falling incomes mean less cash is available. Also, we have discovered that periods of healthy economic growth are nearly always accompanied by year-over-year increases in withheld taxes of at least 5 percent.

Why does the BEA fail to use daily withheld income and employment tax data from the U.S. Treasury to track wages and salaries in near real time? We have asked officials at the BEA this question on numerous occasions. The answer today is the same as it was five years ago when we first began tracking withheld taxes: "Tradition!" The BEA's methodology for calculating personal income is rooted in a tradition stretching back several decades. Someone else's tradition presents us with an opportunity we are happy to exploit. Instead of relying on educated guesses from the BEA, our methodology provides a near real-time measurement of personal income trends. At the same time, the BEA's semiannual and annual revisions to its personal income estimates allow us to compare our estimates with actual data.

We would offer one major caution about personal income data: Robust growth in personal income does not necessarily translate into a rising stock market. When stock prices have surpassed reasonable valuations, rising personal incomes are no guarantee of rising stock prices. For example, during the first quarter of 2004, we estimated that personal income rose 6.4 percent in January, 5.1 percent in February, and 5.2 percent in March. All of these gains exceeded the 5 percent threshold that characterizes a growing economy. Yet the S&P 500 rose only 1.3 percent during this same period. The explanation for this disparity is simple: A massive bubble had formed by the first quarter of 2004. From the end of March 2003 through the end of December 2003, L1 surged an astonishing $97 billion. Over the same period, however, investors poured $139 billion into U.S. equity funds and who knows how much directly into equities. Liquidity theory defines a bubble as a period in which inflows continue rising after L1 has surged. During bubbles, rising personal income does not translate into rising stock prices. Nevertheless, our personal income estimates for the first quarter of 2004 did correctly demonstrate that the U.S. economy was recovering much more strongly than most Wall Street economists were predicting during the first quarter of 2004. Along with other liquidity data, personal income data can help investors make more informed investment decisions.

CORPORATE INCOME

We track corporate income much as we track personal income. Each day, the U.S. Treasury collects income tax payments from companies, which it records in the Daily Treasury Statement. We use corporate income tax payments as a proxy for corporate income just as we use withheld income and employment taxes as a proxy for personal income.

Since companies buy other companies for cash or repurchase their own shares when they see growth ahead, a direct relationship exists between the rise and fall of corporate incomes and L1. A few examples from the most recent recession illustrate this point. In February 2001, corporate income tax payments turned lower year-over-year, and withheld income and employment taxes shifted from high single-digit growth to low single-digit growth. Not surprisingly, L1 turned bearish that month, and the market sold off. In July 2002, both corporate payments and withholdings began to rise year-over-year. At that point, L1 turned bullish again. In fact, the S&P 500 reached a significant bottom during that month. Finally, corporate payments and withholdings fell year-over-year beginning on December 2, 2002, when Venezuela stopped pumping three million barrels a day of heavy oil. Venezuelan production again topped 50 percent of capacity by the third week of January 2003. Beginning on January 23, 2003, corporate payments and withholdings began rising again year-over-year.

Corporate income tax payments are also a highly sensitive indicator of overall economic growth. They rose 98 percent to a record high $235 billion during 2000 from $119 billion during 1999. Not surprisingly, 2000 marked the height of the stock market bubble. During 2001, when the economy slipped into a brief recession, they fell 20 percent to $188 billion, and they declined further to $185 billion during 2002. During 2003, as the economy recovered after the conflict in Iraq, corporate income tax payments increased for the first time since 2000, rising 4.2 percent to $193 billion. As a proxy for corporate income, corporate income tax payments reflect both the ability of companies to buy other companies for cash and repurchase their own shares and the health of the U.S. economy as a whole.

The use of corporate income tax data becomes problematic when frequent changes are made to the rate of corporate taxation, which occurred during 2003 and 2004. These changes are often quite convoluted, so it is difficult to construct a year-over-year comparative model of corporate income.

EMPLOYMENT GROWTH

The labor market is one of the most important indicators of the health of the U.S. economy. As payrolls expand, personal income tends to rise, and more money is available for investment in the stock and bond markets. Conversely, as payrolls contract, personal income tends to fall, and less money is available for investment in the financial markets. Changing employment trends mark the initial and final stages of economic downturns and recoveries. Moreover, the monthly unemployment rate has great psychological significance. It is the most widely reported economic statistic and the only one to which many Americans pay much attention.

The U.S. Bureau of Labor Statistics (BLS), an agency of the U.S.

Department of Labor, reports monthly employment growth in its *Employment Situation Summary* on the first Friday of each month. This report is carefully scrutinized on Wall Street. Like the BEA's monthly personal income estimates, however, the BLS's monthly employment estimates suffer from methodological difficulties. To generate its estimates, the BLS conducts a survey of 400,000 private and government establishments. Then it computes employment, hours, and earnings by industry and geographic region. Finally, it seasonally adjusts the data to normalize trends. During periods of healthy economic growth, these seasonal adjustments work fairly well. At peaks and troughs in the business cycle, however, they tend to overstate or understate changes in employment.

Our monthly estimates of employment growth are based on the raw data the BLS releases, but we use a different methodology to produce our estimates. Instead of seasonally adjusting the data as the BLS does, we analyze the non–seasonally adjusted data on a year-over-year basis. To determine whether the labor market is improving or deteriorating, we examine whether the total number of employees in a particular month is higher or lower than it was in the same month a year earlier. In analyzing the past 35 years of employment data, we have noticed that seasonal variations in employment are highly predictable. In a healthy economy experiencing robust growth, year-over-year improvements typically average 2 percent to 4 percent. For example, employment growth averaged 2.25 percent from 1994 through 1999. As the 2001 recession began, these growth trends reversed. Between 2001 and 2002, employment fell 1.5 percent, and between 2002 and 2003, employment fell another 0.3 percent. Figure 13.2 plots the trend of total U.S. nonfarm employment using non–seasonally adjusted data from January 2001 through December 2003.

Comparing employment from 2001 through 2003 presents a clear picture of how employment declined by nearly 2.8 million employees during these years. Note that the seasonal patterns of employment were roughly the same each year: Employment rose during the first six months of the year, declined somewhat during the summer months, and then recovered before tapering off through the end of the year. By quantifying seasonal patterns rather than attempting to adjust them out of the data, we can more accurately assess employment trends.

When the economy moves from contraction to expansion or vice versa, BLS seasonal adjustments mask rapid declines and rapid increases in employment. More specifically, we believe that as the economy shifts from contraction to expansion, the seasonal adjustments to the BLS data understate improvements in employment by 30 percent to 40 percent. Conversely, as the economy shifts from expansion to contraction, the seasonal adjustments to the BLS data understate deterioration in employment by

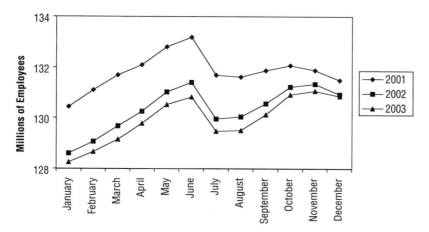

FIGURE 13.2 Total U.S. Nonfarm Employment (Non–Seasonally Adjusted Data), January 2001 to December 2003
Source: TrimTabs Investment Research, U.S. Bureau of Labor Statistics.

roughly the same percentages. Analyzing non–seasonally adjusted BLS employment data on a year-over-year basis provides a more accurate measurement of employment growth than the BLS's seasonally adjusted data.

ONLINE JOB POSTINGS

Our monthly employment estimates provide a snapshot of the labor market, which is a crucial indicator of the health of the U.S. economy. Unfortunately this snapshot arrives only once a month. We could rely entirely on weekly initial unemployment claims data, which the U.S. Department of Labor releases every Thursday. While we do track this data, one-time events—such as the California grocery strike in late 2003—often distort the figures. Also, the number of people claiming first-time unemployment benefits is not necessarily a reliable indicator of companies' demand for labor. We would much rather assess the strength of labor demand directly rather than infer it from how many people are claiming initial unemployment benefits.

To track the labor market on a more real-time basis, we created the TrimTabs Online Job Postings Index. To generate this index, we survey a variety of job posting web sites and gather information on the number of job postings. There are no one-time events to distort this data, and we have found that it provides a reasonably good leading indicator of companies' demand for labor. Figure 13.3 plots the trend of the TrimTabs Online Job Postings Index from March 2001 through December 2003.

What is striking about this graph is the plunge in postings from 115 in early March 2001 to 30 in early January 2002. Not surprisingly, the four-week moving average of weekly initial unemployment claims climbed steadily, rising from about 370,000 claims in early March 2001 to more than 460,000 claims in early October 2001. The index also demonstrates the persistent weakness in the labor market during 2002 and 2003. During this period, the index never rose much above 30. Immediately before the outbreak of hostilities in Iraq in March 2003, postings bottomed at 24. Finally, as postings rose steadily beginning in June 2003, weekly initial unemployment claims dropped from more than 430,000 claims in early June 2003 to just over 350,000 claims at the end of December 2003.

Obviously the TrimTabs Online Job Postings Index does not cover every source of job postings available on the Internet. Also, service positions account for the overwhelming majority of online job postings; manufacturing positions are conspicuously absent. Finally, many positions are simply not posted on the Internet, and still more are not advertised anywhere. Nevertheless, this index provides a sensitive and reasonably broad sample of labor market demand. Since it is calculated daily, its timeliness far outweighs its lack of comprehensiveness. Over the period

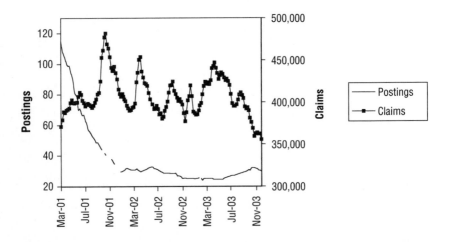

FIGURE 13.3 TrimTabs Online Job Postings Index versus Four-Week Moving Average of Weekly Initial Unemployment Claims, March 2001 to December 2003
Source: TrimTabs Investment Research, U.S. Department of Labor.

we have tracked it, it has proven to be a reliable leading indicator of employment trends.

TRIMTABS PERSONAL INCOME AND TRIMTABS U.S. EMPLOYMENT UPDATE

If you are an institutional investor or a high-net-worth individual who would like access to the latest data on the income and employment indicators described in this chapter, two publications analyze them on a regular basis. *TrimTabs Personal Income* is a weekly publication that focuses on personal income and corporate income. In addition, it analyzes various money supply, debt, and sentiment indicators. Taken together, this data provides a comprehensive forecast of the liquidity available for investment in U.S. financial markets. *TrimTabs U.S. Employment Update* appears each month immediately after the BLS releases its monthly employment report. In addition to our proprietary employment data, each issue analyzes other employment indicators—including weekly initial unemployment claims, help-wanted advertising, announced layoff trends, demand for temporary workers, and manufacturing and service sector employment trends—to forecast overall U.S. employment trends. Both of these publications are edited by Madeline Schnapp, a senior research analyst at TrimTabs Investment Research who specializes in identifying emerging trends that significantly impact financial markets. We also offer a condensed version of our personal income and employment data to individual investors in *TrimTabs Monthly Liquidity*.

CHAPTER 14

How Liquidity Could Save the Markets

L iquidity theory offers more than just a way for investors to beat the stock market casino. Widespread adoption of liquidity theory could transform the nature of the stock market casino itself in ways that would benefit both the house (public companies) and the players (investors). This chapter details simple, low-cost reforms that could level the playing field for individual investors. It also describes how wider use of liquidity theory would mitigate the destructive boom-bust cycles of the equity markets, ultimately improving the quality of life for millions of people.

SOME MODEST PROPOSALS

Several simple, low-cost reforms could provide investors with timely data that would make analysis of each of the liquidity trim tabs—L1, L2, and L3—much more precise. Armed with more timely data, investors would be able to make better decisions in managing their stock market investments.

Net Change in the Trading Float of Shares (L1)

First, we propose that all companies listed on major exchanges issue timely data on the net change in the trading float of their shares as it occurs. This data could be posted in an electronic filing of no more than one page, and quarterly summaries could be included in annual 10-K filings (audited reports of year-end financial results and operations) and quarterly 10-Q filings (unaudited reports updating 10-K filings) that the U.S. Securities and Exchange Commission (SEC) already requires for public companies. This data would break down the trading float into several components:

1. *Actual stock buybacks.* Companies would be required to report the number of shares they actually buy back within 48 hours. Companies currently report actual stock buybacks quarterly. If we had real-time data on actual buybacks, we could generate far more precise estimates of buyback activity rather than relying on the dollar amount and number of new buyback announcements to estimate actual buybacks.

2. *Options conversions.* Companies would be required to report how many stock options all of their directors, officers, and employees exercise and sell each week. With the exception of top executives, this filing need not list the names and titles of sellers—what is important is how many shares were sold and for how much money. Exercises of stock options, which are restricted securities issued through private placements exempt from registration with the SEC, have the same liquidity impact as secondary offerings, since they increase the trading float of shares of companies that are already public.

   The SEC currently requires major insiders—officers, directors, and holders of more than 10 percent of a company's outstanding shares—to file Form 144 (Report of Proposed Sale of Securities) to report exercises of stock options no later than the date on which they intend to sell the shares. The filing of Form 144 does not necessarily mean the sale was actually completed. Also, Form 144 is not required to be filed when the amount of stock intended for sale during any three-month period does not exceed 500 shares and the aggregate sale value does not exceed $10,000.

   In the weekly reporting we propose, we would permit no exemptions for smaller exercises of stock options and exercises of stock options by employees who are not officers, directors, or major holders. Again, we are not interested in sellers' names, just in the number of shares and dollar amounts sold. The cost to companies of providing this information weekly would be inconsequential compared to the benefit shareholders would gain from more timely and complete information about insider transactions.

3. *Insider selling.* Companies would be required to report how many shares all insiders sell each week, just as they would be required to report exercises of stock options. Major insiders—officers, directors, and holders of more than 10 percent of a company's outstanding shares—are currently required to file Form 4 (Statement of Changes in Beneficial Ownership of Securities) with the SEC when they buy or sell stock or exercise stock options. The deadline for filing Form 4 is the tenth

day of the month following the transaction. All transactions of $10,000 or less during a month and all gifts of stock are exempt from this reporting requirement. In the weekly reporting we propose, we would require companies to disclose the total number of shares sold by all insiders, not just major insiders, and we would permit no exemptions for smaller transactions and gifts of stock.

The reporting of stock buyback activity and insider selling activity within 48 hours of transactions would require administrative resources so investors could access this information in a central location. While the SEC has received substantial recent increases in its budget—its budget authority more than doubled from $377 million in 2000 to $812 million in 2004—much of the additional funding has been directed to enforcement because of the corporate malfeasance uncovered during the past three years. If the SEC is unable to assume the responsibilities of tracking actual stock buyback and insider selling activity, TrimTabs would be glad to take on the task at no charge to Uncle Sam.

These disclosures would be a boon to investors because the activities they reveal are driven by the self-interest of companies and corporate insiders. When companies are generating more cash than they require to fund their operations, they will retire existing shares in the market and enhance the relative worth of remaining shares for all shareholders, including corporate executives and board members. If the economy appears to be weakening, companies will sell stock to ensure they have sufficient cash to weather a downturn. CFOs are not attempting to manipulate the stock market when they buy or sell their companies' shares. Yet by buying and selling out of self-interest—managing their companies' cash on hand in anticipation of economic changes—their actions have a major impact on the stock market. Similarly, insiders cash out stock options and sell shares of their own companies when they believe cash is more valuable than their own companies' shares. Investors need to know what companies and insiders are doing in a timely manner to make better investment decisions.

U.S. Equity Fund Flows (L2)

We propose that all mutual fund companies be required to disclose flow data for their mutual funds on the day on which flows actually occur. Only 15 percent of funds are currently willing to provide daily funds flow data. While this proposal would be only a small burden to mutual fund companies, it would provide crucial data to investors in a more timely manner. In fact, TrimTabs would be willing to pay the entire cost of providing this data, which would include contacting each and every mutual fund daily.

We would also agree not to disclose daily individual fund and fund family flows until after the end of each month. Finally, we would work with Stanford Graduate School of Business Professor Eric Zitzewitz and the SEC to monitor daily funds flow to ensure that late trading and market timing no longer occur.

By itself, funds flow data is particularly critical at market turning points. For example, after a prolonged sell-off, we typically examine flows to see how heavily fund investors are selling. If they are selling extremely heavily, it could mean a near-term bottom is forming. Also, after major shocks like the crash of 1987 and the September 11 terrorist attacks, timely funds flow data is important to gauge investors' response to events.

Margin Debt (L3)

Currently the New York Stock Exchange (NYSE) releases monthly data on margin debt at its member firms on a delay of nearly one month. We propose that the NYSE release margin debt data on a weekly basis on a delay of one week. In other words, margin debt data for the first week of the month would be released at the end of the second week of the month. As a result, L3 would become a much more useful indicator. Weekly data rather than monthly data would make L3 much more sensitive to changes in the level of speculative activity in the stock market casino. More timely data would allow followers of liquidity theory to incorporate the level of speculative activity more fully into their near-term liquidity forecasts.

BENEFITS OF IMPROVED LIQUIDITY DATA

The proposals we outline here would have several benefits. First, investors would benefit financially from availability of more timely liquidity data. Heavy increases in corporate selling could caution investors, especially those who borrow money on margin to buy stocks. From November 1999 through March 2000, investors borrowed $96 billion to buy equities, much of which flowed into high-flying technology stocks. This 53 percent surge in margin debt occurred even after companies became net sellers of their own shares. If investors at that time had heeded the turn in corporate liquidity, the Nasdaq would not have risen 70 percent to surpass 5,000 in less than five months, and it would not have cratered 78 percent to just above 1,100 over the following 19 months. These proposals would provide followers of liquidity theory with higher investment returns because more comprehensive and timely information would make liquidity forecasts more accurate.

Improved liquidity data would help level the playing field between corporate insiders and ordinary Americans. The proposals we outline would bring far more fundamental fairness to financial markets than any other reforms being considered by regulators, legislators, or companies themselves. While ordinary investors will never have access to the wealth of information that corporate insiders do, improved liquidity data would at least allow investors to infer the prospects of a particular company by monitoring the behavior of CFOs and other corporate insiders. Investors could cut through bland conference calls and slick press releases and invest based on what corporate insiders are actually doing, not on what they are saying. For example, companies that are overly generous in allocating stock options, whether to top executives or to other employees, increase the number of shares available for trading. The inflated trading floats of these stocks render them more susceptible to market downturns. Conversely, the stocks of companies that grant fewer stock options are cushioned from market downturns, and they benefit more when the market rises. If companies are indifferent to the impact of stock options on their stock performance, investors using liquidity theory could react accordingly.

Most importantly, wider use of liquidity theory would reduce the volatility of the equity markets. If investors paid greater attention to liquidity (objective measurements of the supply and demand for shares) rather than earnings, which can be easily manipulated by shady accounting, the most extreme swings in the market would be reduced. How exactly would this work? Let's return to the technology bubble in late 1999 and early 2000. If more investors had been following liquidity theory, they would have known that corporate America became a net seller in November 1999. They would have recognized that new offerings were exploding. They would have been warned that corporate insiders were practically falling all over one another in their rush to cash out unlocking stock options. If more investors had been following liquidity theory, there is no way U.S. equity fund inflows would have reached a whopping $26 billion per month between October 1999 to April 2000, and there is no way margin debt would have popped 53 percent between November 1999 and March 2000. The bubble would have been nowhere near as large, and the resulting bust would have been nowhere near as painful.

History shows that wild booms are always followed by bitter busts. It is the bankruptcies and loss of confidence that occur during these busts—not stock market losses—that truly ravage economies and societies. As discussed in Chapter 1, the hardships of the Great Depression were caused not so much by the crash of 1929 as by bank failures and bankruptcies. The Great Depression, however, is hardly the only example of the destructive effects of busted bubbles.

Consider the Japanese economy over the past quarter century. During the mid-1980s, many Japanese and American investors believed America was losing its competitiveness and that Japan would replace it as the dominant economy in the world. Companies around the world scrambled to adopt Japanese management techniques and production practices. Meanwhile, Japan gradually loosened its monetary policy, which lowered interest rates and increased the money supply. In a process known as *zaitech*, companies obtained low-interest loans, often through the sale of convertible bonds, and used them to speculate in financial markets. In 1985, the Bank of Japan reported that only 12 percent of the 29 trillion yen that Japanese corporations raised was used for capital spending—the remaining 88 percent was used to finance speculative activities. As a result, asset prices surged. Rising asset prices boosted corporate earnings, which in turn encouraged investors to buy more equities, which in turn encouraged the cycle to continue. A substantial percentage of the earnings of the largest Japanese companies in the late 1980s derived purely from market speculation.

Fueled by easy money, the Japanese real estate and stock markets exploded. Land in downtown Tokyo fetched thousands of dollars per square foot, and the land underneath the Imperial Palace in central Tokyo was rumored to be worth more than all of the real estate in California. To slow the boom, the Bank of Japan raised interest rates in May 1989 and December 1989. On December 29, 1989, the Nikkei topped out at 38,916. The Bank of Japan raised interest rates five more times by August 1990, and the stock market bubble began to burst. By August 31, 1990, the Nikkei had already fallen to 25,978, a 33 percent decline from the all-time high it had reached just eight months earlier. Real estate prices began to collapse, and just two and a half years after reaching its all-time high, the Nikkei had sunk to 15,952, a 59 percent decline from its peak. (See Figure 14.1.)

The economic fallout from the busted bubble has lasted more than a decade. From the bursting of the bubble in 1990 through the end of 2003, the Japanese economy was basically stagnant. Annual gross domestic product (GDP) growth in Japan in the 1990s was less than 1 percent compared to about 4 percent in the 1980s. Neither nominal interest rates near zero nor massive budget deficits were enough to prevent the onset of economic contraction and crippling deflation. While nearly all developed economies expanded throughout most of the 1990s, Japan suffered either three or four recessions, depending on one's definition. At the same time, consumer prices turned negative in 1995, recovered briefly in 1996 and 1997, and remained negative from late 1999 to early 2004, the longest bout of deflation a developed economy has experienced since the Great Depression.

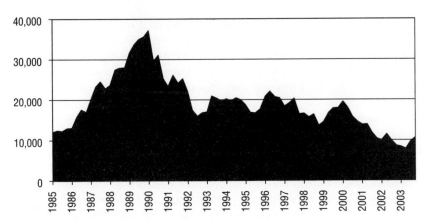

FIGURE 14.1   Nikkei 225, January 1985 to December 2003
Raw data obtained from Yahoo! Finance.

What about bankruptcies? Unlike the United States during the Great Depression, Japan experienced relatively few bankruptcies in the wake of its bubble, which somewhat paradoxically was a major cause of the country's continuing malaise. "Zombie companies" continued to operate despite their insolvency, which merely postponed the restructurings that were essential to restore the economy's health. Bank balance sheets remained crammed with nonperforming loans, sharply limiting the liquidity available for investment despite extremely low nominal interest rates. A substantial proportion of Japan's banking system was insolvent. As a result of successive governments' refusals to confront its economic problems head-on, Japan continued to struggle during the first years of the twenty-first century. While GDP in Japan began rising during the second quarter of 2002, the unemployment rate remained consistently above 5 percent during the first three years of the twenty-first century, its highest level since the end of World War II. On April 28, 2003, the Nikkei hit a 20-year low of 7,607.88. As we write this book, the Nikkei has recovered to about 11,000, but this level is still less than a third of its all-time high.

Who is investing in the Japanese stock market today? For the most part, it is not ordinary Japanese! According to a National Bureau of Economic Research Working Paper by Tokuo Iwaisako in April 2003, the percentage of Japanese who own stocks rose from 26 percent in 1987 to 30 percent in 1990. After the bubble burst, it steadily declined to 24 percent by 1996. It has since remained around this level, even as equity ownership has increased in most other developed nations. The percentage of Japanese household financial wealth held in stocks dropped even more sharply after the bubble burst. After reaching 35 percent in 1990, stock holdings plummeted to 18 percent of household financial wealth in 1993 and just 7 percent in 1999. Ordinary Japanese were so badly burned by the bubble that burst 15 years ago that few own substantial equity investments today. For more than a decade, most Japanese have been content to park their assets in bank deposits earning miserly rates of interest. The bust scared off millions of potential investors. Today Japanese institutional investors and foreigners are the main players in the Japanese stock market.

While the economic pain was nowhere near as severe as Japan's over the past 15 years, the United States suffered considerably after the technology bubble burst in 2000. After investors were no longer willing to throw cash at any company with ".com" at the end of its name and buy IPOs of firms with meager revenues and no earnings, the Nasdaq fell 78 percent from its peak in just 19 months, and more than $7 trillion in wealth was wiped out. The economy dipped into recession, tens of thousands of businesses went bankrupt, and millions of workers lost their jobs. We imagine that few readers of this book do not know someone who was personally affected by the bust. Wealth, businesses, and jobs were not the only things that were lost. Many investors lost confidence in the integrity of corporate America. With soaring profits no longer helping to mask dishonest practices, dirty laundry from the likes of Enron, WorldCom, Global Crossing, Adelphia, and Tyco International found their way into courtrooms across the nation. As a result of the carnage, million of investors vowed to steer clear of the stock market for good, depriving companies of capital for investment. While many Americans have returned to the stock market in 2003 and 2004, others were so badly burned that they are content to sit on the sidelines. If you are among those sitting on the sidelines, we hope the information in this book has given you the knowledge and confidence to get back in the game.

As these examples demonstrate, the economic and social consequences of busted bubbles are devastating. Of course, even better disclosure of corporate trading activities, along with better understanding of liquidity among investors, will never eliminate stock market rallies and tumbles. The stock market will always fluctuate. Yet wider use of liquidity theory among investors would mean lower stock market highs during booms and higher stock market lows during busts. Weaker booms would result in less severe busts, and the bankruptcies and related economic and social dislocations would be greatly reduced. Lower volatility would increase the amount of capital available for investment. Investors would be far more willing to move their cash from low-yielding savings products into the stock market—making it possible for new companies to emerge and existing companies to raise capital—if stock market volatility diminished. Not only would investors enjoy more consistent returns, but corporate America would also benefit from a more consistent supply of capital to expand its operations. These capital improvements would stimulate economic growth and create more jobs, ultimately improving the quality of life for all Americans, even those who do not own stock at all. Everyone would benefit if more investors played the stock market casino on the side of the house.

Following are brief descriptions of the 15 columns of Table A.1.

How to Read the Table

1. Period. Month and/or year of data.
2. S&P 500. Value of S&P 500 at end of period.
3. Market Capitalization. Market value of all NYSE, Nasdaq, and AMEX stocks, excluding American Depositary Receipts. Market Capitalization = All Shares Outstanding × Current Share Prices.
4. **L1 Net Float.** Net change in trading float of shares. Best leading indicator of stock market direction. L1 Net Float = New Offerings + Insider Selling − ⅔ New Cash Takeovers − ⅓ Completed Cash Takeovers − New Stock Buybacks.
5. New Cash Takeovers. Cash portion of newly announced takeovers of public companies.
6. Completed Cash Takeovers. Cash portion of completed acquisitions of public companies.
7. New Stock Buybacks. Dollar value at previous day's close of new stock buyback announcements.
8. New Offerings. Dollar value of new equity offerings sold in the United States, excluding closed-end funds.
9. Insider Selling. Estimated selling by all corporate insiders.
10. Foreign Flow. Net purchases or sales of U.S. stocks by foreigners.
11. All Equity Flow. Flows into and out from U.S. equity funds and global equity funds.
12. **L2 U.S. Equity Funds Flow.** Flows into and out from U.S. equity funds. Lagging contrary indicator.
13. U.S. Equity Funds Total Assets. Total assets of all U.S. equity funds.
14. U.S. Equity Funds Cash Percentage. Percentage of all U.S. equity fund assets held in cash equivalents.
15. **L3 Margin Debt.** Net change in margin debt at New York Stock Exchange member firms. Lagging contrary indicator.

TABLE A.1 Historical Liquidity Data

Period (1)	S&P 500 (2)	Market Cap. (3)	L1 Net Float (4)	New Cash T/O (5)	Comp. Cash T/O (6)	New Buybacks (7)	New Offerings (8)	Insider Selling (9)	Foreign Flow (10)	All Equity Flow (11)	L2 U.S. Equity Flow (12)	Equity Funds Assets (13)	Equity Funds Cash (14)	L3 Margin Debt (15)
1995	616	7.310	−69,208	89,000	82,939	101,114	86,770	32,118	11,240	124,392	112,880	1,053	7.7	15,194
1996	741	8.954	−107,479	71,223	71,382	181,759	98,850	46,706	12,511	216,937	169,421	1,441	6.1	24,220
1997	970	11.560	−40,449	101,146	97,728	133,825	132,592	60,792	65,870	227,107	189,261	2,022	5.8	28,930
1998	1,229	13.860	−101,807	157,342	149,507	105,700	89,974	68,652	53,978	157,032	149,506	2,587	4.7	15,670
1999	1,469	17.619	−69,036	232,949	153,555	174,432	180,303	131,604	107,807	187,666	176,441	3,457	4.2	87,610
2000	1,329	16.396	72,623	235,990	226,290	221,903	259,146	268,140	174,002	309,365	259,571	3,419	5.5	−29,697
Jan–01	1,366	16.890	16,433	13,016	22,654	19,552	13,523	38,688	23,778	24,937	21,448	3,536	5.3	−1,680
Feb–01	1,240	15.290	47,463	7,687	22,542	19,552	42,849	36,800	9,435	−3,285	1,139	3,180	5.6	−10,240
Mar–01	1,160	14.070	18,698	6,473	10,672	12,527	17,896	21,200	7,428	−20,694	−15,760	2,935	5.4	−21,560
Apr–01	1,249	13.656	23,782	5,818	14,709	11,476	16,437	27,600	6,627	19,141	17,254	3,214	5.2	1,730
May–01	1,256	14.247	64,193	14,980	16,665	15,100	50,034	44,800	17,321	18,383	20,839	3,252	5.2	8,320
Jun–01	1,224	13.216	41,738	2,568	5,175	17,619	40,793	22,000	10,438	10,851	9,736	3,198	5.3	−4,180
Jul–01	1,211	12.144	18,234	12,957	6,306	16,645	25,621	20,000	11,475	−1,278	2,434	3,128	5.2	−5,000
Aug–01	1,134	11.564	23,926	6,355	13,475	7,304	15,755	24,200	7,703	−4,953	−1,440	2,940	5.2	−4,120
Sep–01	1,041	10.337	−45,511	13,142	3,678	53,640	7,319	10,800	−11,532	−29,962	−27,263	2,626	5.2	−16,260
Oct–01	1,060	11.134	23,024	1,137	8,357	18,825	25,390	20,000	7,261	873	5,140	2,710	5.3	−50
Nov–01	1,139	11.781	11,501	2,781	6,434	21,314	26,061	10,752	13,172	15,152	13,381	2,925	5.3	4,640
Dec–01	1,148	11.147	17,091	6,975	18,392	24,121	35,389	16,600	13,284	2,802	6,822	2,989	4.9	1,800
2001	1,148	14.435	260,572	93,889	149,059	237,675	317,067	293,440	116,390	31,966	53,570	2,989	4.9	−46,600
Jan–02	1,130	14.192	19,955	632	4,693	5,942	20,282	7,600	8,608	19,350	16,011	2,949	5.2	1,500
Feb–02	1,107	13.797	8,826	331	5,291	18,780	19,737	9,852	2,167	4,691	7,554	2,889	5.2	−3,360
Mar–02	1,147	14.392	30,714	5,064	1,748	1,973	31,398	5,248	6,854	29,662	26,714	3,050	4.9	2,340
Apr–02	1,077	13.656	15,667	3,889	3,560	6,910	19,156	7,200	7,769	12,859	12,200	2,924	5.2	1,570
May–02	1,067	14.247	27,391	5,856	4,611	5,189	26,821	11,200	−314	4,838	2,726	2,894	4.9	−80
Jun–02	990	13.216	6,982	1,177	3,536	22,337	25,582	5,700	4,045	−18,247	−18,946	2,662	4.5	−4,590
Jul–02	912	12.144	−8,836	1,301	2,302	25,719	12,817	5,700	9,653	−52,608	−49,011	2,386	4.4	−10,110

	(2)	(3)	(4)	(5)	(6)	(7)	(8)	(9)	(10)	(11)	(12)	(13)	(14)	(15)
Aug–02	916	11.564	−8,985	1,584	1,470	13,964	875	5,650	4,614	−3,110	−610	2,399	4.9	−3,360
Sep–02	815	10.377	3,209	2,775	954	7,018	7,546	4,850	−6,466	−16,051	−14,455	2,163	4.9	−2,590
Oct–02	886	11.134	−3,769	2,476	2,610	15,649	10,701	3,700	3,616	−7,576	−7,335	2,300	4.8	320
Nov–02	936	11.781	−33	3,110	3,789	19,419	14,622	8,100	6,480	6,907	6,251	2,441	4.8	2,490
Dec–02	880	11.147	−174	7,644	1,125	6,554	8,003	3,850	2,416	−8,381	−5,944	2,305	4.4	1,320
2002	880	11.147	87,087	35,839	35,689	149,454	197,540	78,650	47,058	−27,665	−24,847	2,305	4.4	−15,870
Jan–03	856	10.886	−8,892	2,425	6,863	22,518	14,179	3,350	−2,796	−262	−1,319	2,245	4.4	530
Feb–03	841	10.634	−4,447	3,445	3,184	12,654	7,765	3,800	−2,078	−10,886	−10,384	2,196	4.2	−880
Mar–03	848	10.665	−3,951	2,088	1,395	16,017	7,723	6,200	2,840	42	1,414	2,217	4.6	1,900
Apr–03	917	11.571	2,344	6,319	2,857	7,731	13,141	6,000	4,357	16,115	12,561	2,402	4.8	30
May–03	964	12.830	21,764	2,148	1,885	6,650	24,874	14,000	6,593	11,919	12,456	2,566	4.6	5,930
Jun–03	975	13.020	21,756	9,780	1,356	6,599	25,830	9,500	10,308	18,643	18,070	2,628	4.6	2,170
Jul–03	990	13.290	6,382	8,813	1,473	17,187	24,538	5,400	−7,863	21,473	19,042	2,709	4.4	−100
Aug–03	1,008	13.597	12,571	2,580	1,398	5,680	9,937	10,500	11,585	23,605	18,815	2,803	4.3	1,210
Sep–03	996	13.533	11,720	4,086	1,580	13,193	19,765	8,400	−6,225	17,501	17,154	2,785	4.3	6,210
Oct–03	1,051	14.360	2,878	7,961	1,312	11,775	15,400	5,000	−1,244	25,022	19,188	2,967	4.4	6,850
Nov–03	1,058	14.620	22,451	667	1,194	7,631	18,924	12,000	8,779	14,928	12,532	3,031	4.4	9,400
Dec–03	1,112	15.280	−2,946	8,340	2,339	26,219	17,815	11,800	13,330	14,178	9,343	3,167	4.0	1,080
2003	1,112	15.280	93,930	58,652	26,836	153,854	199,891	95,950	45,416	152,278	127,257	3,167	4.0	34,330
Jan–04	1,131	15.540	−2,659	2,375	2,590	24,877	16,265	8,400	12,787	42,948	31,447	3,261	4.2	5,600
Feb–04	1,145	15.760	−6,514	37,663	4,225	22,013	28,027	14,000	2,408	26,150	18,136	3,331	4.2	1,540
Mar–04	1,126	15.530	31,696	9,408	910	6,980	32,254	13,000	−13,461	15,520	9,752	3,314	4.0	−650
Apr–04	1,107	15.121	1,343	6,311	2,823	18,963	15,855	9,600	−1,891	22,990	15,993	3,251	4.1	1,570
May–04	1,121	15.301	−7,067	20,403	2,867	22,907	20,204	10,200	−7,623	427	−919	3,294	3.9	−2,810
Jun–04	1,141	15.730	4,682	8,704	4,617	14,921	18,546	8,400	1,904	10,397	7,612	3,377	4.0	1,620
Jul–04	1,102	15.183	−31,023	7,618	3,693	46,045	12,533	8,800	9,778	9,462	6,500	3,240	4.0	−3,060
Aug–04	1,104	15.354	−17,093	21,617	15,427	15,328	11,392	6,400	−2,084	1,089	−1,214	3,240	4.1	70
Sep–04	1,115	15.671	−2,684	12,494	1,783	16,850	16,793	6,300	−3,830	10,113	6,001	3,332	4.1	3,000
2004	1,115	15.671	−29,318	126,593	38,935	188,884	171,869	85,100	−2,012	140,322	94,782	3,332	4.1	6,880

Source: (2) Yahoo! Finance; (3) to (8) TrimTabs Investment Research; (9) Thomson Financial; (10) U.S. Department of the Treasury; (11) to (14) Investment Company Institute; (15) New York Stock Exchange.

About the Authors

Charles Biderman is the founder and president of TrimTabs Investment Research. Born in New York City, he earned a BA from Brooklyn College and an MBA from Harvard Business School. He began his career as Alan Abelson's assistant at *Barron's* from 1971 to 1973. After correctly predicting the collapse of real estate investment trusts, he became a successful real estate entrepreneur, putting together various deals in Tennessee and New Jersey. He founded TrimTabs in 1990 to provide portfolio managers and market strategists with unique investment insights. He is frequently quoted in the financial media, including the *Wall Street Journal*, *Barron's*, CNBC, and Bloomberg.

David Santschi is an editorial consultant and copy editor with TrimTabs Investment Research. Born in Cincinnati, he earned an AB in history magna cum laude with high honors from Davidson College and an MA in history from the University of Wisconsin–Madison. Currently he is a doctoral candidate in early modern European history at the University of Wisconsin–Madison.

Index

A

Abelson, Alan, 23–24, 26
Accounting fraud, 65–67
Acquisitions, 54, 64
Adelphia, 178
Amazon.com, 3
American Association of
    Individual Investors Investor
    Sentiment Survey, 154
American depositary receipts
    (ADRs), 76
Ameritrade, 47, 100
AMG Data Services, 85
Analyst recommendations, 13,
    16, 66–67
Arbitrageurs, 45, 72
Arnold, Daniel A., 116
Asian currency crisis, 56
AT&T Wireless, 43, 71–72,
    119–120

B

Baby boomer generation, 116
Balance sheets, 54, 65
Bank of Japan, 176

Bankruptcies, 18–19, 26, 175,
    177–179
Barclays Global Investors:
    functions of, generally,
    128
    iShares ETFs, 133,
    141–142
Barron's, 23–24, 85
Bear market:
    characterized, 12, 14, 16–18,
    20, 30, 38, 46–48, 60,
    93
    development of, 113–116
Beardstown Ladies, 12
Berman, Meyer, 24
Biderman, Charles, 19, 23, 117,
    156, 185
Blodget, Henry, 13, 62
Bloomberg News, 80
Bombay Sensex, 5–6
Brokerage firm(s):
    commissions, 1, 36, 62, 142
    functions of, 17, 29, 36–37,
    46, 62, 105
    online brokers, 100
Buffett, Warren, 21
Bull! A History of the Boom
    (Mahar), 101

187